<CODING PROJECTS FOR ALL>

# CODE A
# MINECRAFT™
# MOD
# IN
# JAVASCRIPT
# STEP
# BY
# STEP

JOSHUA ROMPHF

Rosen
**YA**™

New York

Published in 2020 by The Rosen Publishing Group, Inc.
29 East 21st Street, New York, NY 10010

Copyright © 2020 by The Rosen Publishing Group, Inc.

First Edition

**Library of Congress Cataloging-in-Publication Data**

Names: Romphf, Joshua, author.
Title: Code a Minecraft mod in JavaScript step by step / Joshua Romphf.
Description: First edition. | New York : Rosen Publishing, 2020. | Series:
Coding projects for all | Includes bibliographical references and index.
Identifiers: LCCN 2018057373| ISBN 9781725340206 (library bound) | ISBN
9781725340152 (pbk.)
Subjects: LCSH: Computer games—Programming—Juvenile literature. |
JavaScript (Computer program language)—Juvenile literature. | Minecraft
(Game)—Juvenile literature.
Classification: LCC QA76.76.C672 R645 2020 | DDC 794.8/1525—dc23
LC record available at https://lccn.loc.gov/2018057373

*Manufactured in the United States of America*

# CONTENTS

# INTRODUCTION

**M**inecraft. You know it. You love it. And you're not alone! Since Markus "Notch" Persson and his company, Mojang, officially released the game in 2011, it has rocketed to the top of the gaming world—and stayed there for longer than anyone ever thought possible.

How does a game stay so popular for so long? One answer is simple: great gameplay. Another answer? The modding community. *Minecraft* is a game based on infinite creativity, and modifying the game—to make custom blocks, new levels, or anything else—has kept the experience fresh and fun for tens of millions of loyal fans.

What better way to learn about computer science than working with your favorite game? There are some amazing tools out there that let beginner programmers (hint: that's you) make awesome mods for *Minecraft*. Luckily enough, you hold in your hands the key to unlocking those tools and using your creativity to code and publish your very own *Minecraft* mods using the programming language JavaScript.

The first section will mostly contain pen-and-paper or pseudocode exercises, covering the more language-agnostic concepts we'll be using throughout the book. Woah, woah, I know throwing around phrases like "language-agnostic" this early is kind of scary. What that means, really, is that these concepts can be applied to many different programming languages—not just JavaScript. I'm a firm believer that the fundamentals of programming are useful no matter what language (or languages!) you learn. If you're able to learn the ins and outs of one language—like JavaScript—it's going to be a lot easier when you try to grasp the nuances and features of another. So with this in mind, we're going to go ahead and start with some baseline building blocks. We'll go through a brief introduction on how computers and programming languages work, followed by some language fundamentals, such as syntax and semantics. Then, we'll start to think about all of the different types of data that our programs work with. Finally, we'll get into the core logical concepts of programs and how they flow. Get your pen and paper ready!

Don't worry—once you're a master of the basics, we'll get into making your first awesome mod. The next section will show you the ropes of JavaScript more specifically. You'll learn about classes, variables, and more. I'm also going to give you a rundown on using ScriptCraft, a custom tool for translating all your new JavaScript knowledge into *Minecraft*.

Chapter three is where the fun really begins. Here, you'll start putting your knowledge to good use, making a mod I like to call the Cellar Dweller. This mod has it all: randomly generated dungeons, awesome enemies, and some pretty sweet loot to boot. I'm also going to walk you through publishing and documenting all your hard work for all the world (or just your friends) to see.

It's going to be a wild ride!

# Chapter One

# HOW PROGRAMMING LANGUAGES WORK

**B**efore you can get started with programming exercises and building awesome stuff with JavaScript, it's probably a good idea to know a little bit about how programming languages work in general.

You know what a computer is—you probably use one every day! But do you ever stop to think about how it works? At a basic level, computers are electromechanical machines that can take instructions from humans and do a lot of different things with them. People write programs—or software—to communicate with the electromechanical pieces, or hardware. Everything you do on a computer has some sort of programming behind it, from surfing the internet, to sending an e-mail, to playing *Minecraft*.

Though they're capable of doing some unbelievable stuff, computers can understand only very straightforward and limited instructions. In fact, they can understand only 1s and 0s. This is called binary. It works like this: when a computer sees a 1, it knows to turn an electrical pulse on; when it sees a 0, it knows to turn that electricity off. Based on the order and length of these binary instructions, the hardware does different things.

The instructions that are sent directly to the computer's central processing unit, or CPU, are known as machine code. Machine code is the lowest form of binary communication between a human and a computer. That doesn't mean it's bad—in computer science, the "lower" a code is, the closer it is to machine code. The "higher" it is, the closer it is to human language.

Why does this matter to you? Because I'm sure you don't really want to type "01101000 01100101 01101100 01101100 01101111" just to say "hello"! In the early days of digital computing, though, programmers had to write instructions for their hardware just like this—using binary. These instructions were actually punched onto a piece of paper and fed into the computer. Phew, sounds awful, doesn't it?

When people wanted to execute complex tasks on a computer, they realized that they would need to use languages that were easier for humans to read and write. Only supernerds would really want to type everything in machine code. The result was Assembly Language, which is a set of more human-readable instructions that are converted to machine code. Still, early computer scientists wanted more. After all, why should a human have to learn the language of a machine when he or she could just design the machine to understand human language?

Most software developers and programmers use higher-level languages that are closer to human, or natural, languages. That allows them to do more complicated things while typing significantly less code. Think about it like this: you could probably write a lot using English, but what if I asked you to do it in Latin?

High-level code might be easy for humans to understand, but a CPU can read only machine code. So how does the language get translated? That's where interpreters and compilers come in.

A compiler directly translates high-level code to native machine code. That means it produces code that can communicate directly with the CPU. Compiled code is usually faster for this reason—the distance between the code and the processor is pretty small!

On the other hand, an interpreter will compile the code to an intermediate format that's called byte code. Then, it will execute each line as machine code at runtime (when the program is actually running), versus at compile time (when the program is being compiled, or translated).

So, what does that all mean? In short, compiled code can be very useful when you want to make programs that are high performance and can run really quickly. Similarly, compilers can check for—and catch—bugs in your program before you even run it! Sounds great, right?

Interpreted code, on the other hand, can be a lot more dynamic. For instance, it can be cross-platform (meaning it will work on Mac or Windows, for example) and you can actually modify the code while it's running!

Okay, so why do you need to know any of this to program a *Minecraft* mod? Why am I trying to bore you to tears? Well, it's important to know that ScriptCraft uses JavaScript to create mods, and, in this case, your JavaScript code will be interpreted, not compiled. That means that you'll be able to write code directly in *Minecraft* and watch as things change right before your eyes!

JavaScript is one of the most popular programming languages in the world because it can run on so many devices (in web browsers, on phones, on servers, and more) and it does not need to be compiled before you run it.

# On and Off

 1    10–15 minutes    Paper, pencil

## Activity Overview

Because everything in the digital world is binary, the space that your data takes up (on the file system or in memory) is also represented in binary. In this activity, you're going to do a bit of binary counting. That sounds pretty tough, but it's actually a lot easier than it looks!

Check out the image below. Starting with the box on the far right, notice how each number is multiplied by 2 as you move left. All of these boxes are in the "on" state. As they are below, the total sum of the boxes is 31. If you wanted to change that sum, you would have to cover up some of the boxes—which would switch them to an "off" state.

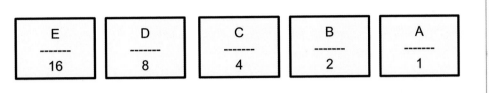

This may seem a little weird, but here's an example. If you cover up all of the boxes except for A, the sum will be 1. Using 1s and 0s—on and off—to represent our states, a sum of 1 would look like this: 00001. What about a sum of 2? Well, that would be 00010. And how about 3? It's 00011. Holy cow, you just counted in binary without even knowing it!

## Instructions

Based on the image above, try to come up with the binary sequence for every number from 1 to 31. If you get stuck, just remember that you can physically cover up the numbers you don't need with a finger. You can then write out the sequence based on which box is blocked, or "off."

# High to Low

 2   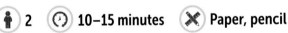 10–15 minutes    Paper, pencil

## Activity Overview

High-level programming languages were invented so that programmers could spend their time solving problems, rather than writing extremely complex instructions. Low-level languages have to tell a computer exactly what to do, step by step, while high-level languages often combine several smaller steps into a single line that is much easier to understand. You're probably wondering how this process works!

# Instructions

Start off by finding a friend and deciding which person is going to play a high-level language and which person is going to play a low-level language. The one who is going to be the high-level language will write a simple instruction on a piece of paper. This could be anything! You'll probably want to start with an everyday task, like "get ready for bed" or "turn on the light." Once that player has the task written down, it's the other player's turn. The low-level language should write out every individual step involved in the initial instruction. For example, a low-level version of "turn on the light" might be:

1. Stand up.
2. Take ten steps toward the light switch.
3. Raise your right arm.
4. Flip the light switch up.

Take a few turns passing instructions back and forth before switching roles.

# Language Fundamentals

Before you start writing any JavaScript, you're going to want to understand some of the core concepts of the language. Throughout the course of the book, you'll find that we keep coming back to these concepts. In fact, the more you program, the more you'll notice that a lot of these features are shared across many different languages!

Believe it or not, you really don't have to be a science or math whiz to get into programming. Because computers are so advanced and affordable nowadays, anybody can learn how to program, either by teaching himself or herself or taking classes. Don't get me wrong—programming can be a challenge. But it's important not to get discouraged! Sometimes you'll get frustrated, but you just need to step back, take a break, and come back to it later. The activities in the following sections are designed to ease you into the process. No need to be intimidated—just stay curious, have fun, and you'll be programming in *Minecraft* in no time!

# Hello, Operator: Syntax, Operators, and Operands

Remember how I mentioned how the higher level the programming language is, the closer it is to how humans communicate? The technical term for this is a language's syntax, which refers to how the language is structured. Syntax also describes what rules and symbols are allowed within it.

Think about the English language. There are a lot of rules you have to follow in order to communicate. Although it may be pretty fun, you can't just make up words or randomly jumble up a sentence and expect other people to understand you. The same can be said for programming languages. A compiler or interpreter responsible for translating a program expects it to follow a very specific set of rules. If you don't structure your program within those rules, you'll get errors.

The same is true for symbols in an programming language. While it would be really cool if you could make up your own letters and add them to the English alphabet, nobody would understand what you were trying to write or say! The symbols, in other words, are all of the different characters a specific language allows you to use.

To be more specific, here is an example of some basic symbols that we will see a lot of throughout the book:

- () parentheses (left and right)
- {} curly brackets (left and right)
- [] square brackets (left and right)
- & ampersand

- : colon
- ; semicolon
- ' single quote
- " double quote
- / forward slash
- _ underscore
- − dash
- \ backslash
- | pipe
- > greater than
- < less than

Depending on the language, a compiler or interpreter may not allow certain symbols, or the rules may not permit their use in a certain place. When this happens, you are usually met with something called a syntax error. Get ready to see that error a lot! It's the most common bug for beginner programmers.

This is beginning to sound a little bit like your English classes, isn't it? Since these are programming *languages* we're talking about, there are a lot of concepts borrowed from human languages. Just as programming and natural languages have syntax (structural rules), they also follow semantics. In natural language, semantics is the meaning of a sentence. The same can be applied to programming languages. Semantics refers to the actual instructions that the compiler or interpreter has to translate to machine code. In other words: what the program actually means!

A program can be syntactically correct, but semantically incorrect. This means it can likely compile—and possibly even run—but there is some flawed logic in it. And that's bad! Usually, this takes the form of runtime bugs that happen when a program tries to access resources that aren't available to it, add a word and a number together, or something else that just isn't right.

What does this look like in natural language? It may come in the form of a sentence that is grammatically fine but makes no sense. A famous example is "colorless green ideas sleep furiously." Who the heck can figure that mess out? Semantic errors in natural language don't have to be that weird, either. They could just be sentences that express a meaning that is false or could be the result of something as simple as misplacing a comma.

What about this other famous one? "The panda eats, shoots, and leaves." Well, it's syntactically correct, but the meaning is wrong. Have you ever seen a shooting panda? I didn't think so. They don't actually do that—they just eat shoots and leaves. As you learn to program, you will encounter a lot of semantic errors. They won't be nearly as fun as these examples from the English language. They're a lot harder to track down than syntax errors, but with a little patience, you should be able to figure them out.

Okay, so you know that programs have rules that they must follow, and they need to produce instructions that express a valid meaning for the compiler. But how do you actually start to write code?

Think about programs in very simple terms: you write them in order to perform some type of operation on some type of data. Throughout this book, you'll notice that your programs will all do something with whatever type of information we feed into them. That sounds pretty easy—for the coder, anyway. You know how to tell the difference between the "data" and the "doing something." But how does a compiler or interpreter know that there's a difference?

Like the English language, nearly all programming languages (except for some super obscure ones, but who needs those?) are written from left to right. That's just like how you read and write sentences. In programming languages, however, there are operators and operands that help the computer understand what to do with each line of code. These are concepts that are borrowed from math, and many should look familiar to you.

The operand refers to the data that you would like to perform some type of operation on, while the operator refers to the actual operation. Take this simple arithmetic:

$$1 + 2 = 3$$

In this example, "1" and "2" are operands, and the "+" is the addition operator. Here's another example:

$$9 / 3 = 3$$

In this example, "9" and "3" are operands and the "/" is the division operator.

What makes most programming languages unique, though, is the "=" (equal) symbol and where it is positioned. If you wrote a program that consisted only of the line "9 / 3 = 3," you would get a syntax error. This's because the equal symbol is used for assignment. That assignment operator is likely the most important operator you'll use throughout your programs.

When you're doing arithmetic like the expressions above, you're computing the result and putting it on the right side of the equal symbol. That's easy to do on paper, but when you're programming, you need to reserve some space in memory to store the computed result. If you don't, you'll lose it! What the assignment operator does is specify that you want to store the result of the operation in memory and that you want to be able to access it in the future.

The mathematical expression "9 / 3 = 3" would actually look something more like this if you put it in programming terms:

$$result = 9 / 3$$

Where "result" is the answer to the division operation stored in memory.

Do you feel any different? More accomplished? Well, you should! You just learned about your first variable. A variable is a reference to some storage space in memory, which you can then access in your program by calling its name, or label. Based on the expression above, you would get access to the value of the division operation by calling on your "result" variable. This is the most basic way of passing information around in a program.

How does knowing about variables change your understanding of operators and operands? In programming, we often refer to left and right operands. In the case of our expression above, we could label the operators and operands like this:

result = 9 / 3

Where "result" is the left operand; the equal symbol is the assignment operator; and the expression "9 / 3" is the right operand of the assignment operator. And if we want to get really specific "9" is the left operand of the "/" operator; and "3" is the right operand of the "/" operator.

Confused? Well, one thing that may help is that you can use parentheses () when performing mathematical operations, and the program will follow to the order of operations you've probably learned about in your math class.

Most languages have a stock set of arithmetic operators that you can work with. Here are the ones that you'll likely see the most, with explanations:

- Addition: +
    Used to add the left operand to the right operand
    Example: 1 + 1 (2)
- Subtraction: -
    Used to subtract the right operand from the left operand
    Example: 2 - 1 (1)
- Multiplication: *
    Used to multiply the left operand by the right operand
    Example: 2 * 2 (4)
- Division: /
    Used to divide the left operand by the right operand
    Example: 4 / 2 (2)

- Increment: ++
    Used to increase a value by 1. This is what you'd call a unary operator. That's just a fancy way of saying that it's an operator that works with only one operand (see below).
    Example:
        myNumber = 1
        myNumber++ (2)
- Decrement: --
    Used to decrease a value by 1; also a unary operator.
    Example:
        myNumber = 3
        myNumber-- (2)
- Remainder (Modulo): %
    Used to get the remainder from a division operation between the left and right operands.
    Example:
        2 % 2 (0)
        3 % 2 (1)
        13 % 5 (3)
- Negation:
    Used to provide the negative value of a number; also a unary operator.
    Example:
        myNumber = 3
        -myNumber (-3)
        myOtherNumber = -5
        -myOtherNumber (5)
- Exponentiation: **
    Used to calculate the base (left operand) to the exponent (right operand) power. The equivalent of base$^{exponent}$
    Example:
        2 ** 4 (16)
        3 ** 1 (3)

# Syntactically Correct

👤 2   🕐 5–10 minutes   ✗ Paper, pencil

## Activity Overview

This activity will help you to grasp the importance of syntax to programming. You've got to really understand what a syntax error is before you can identify one in your code!

## Instructions

To start off, find a friend. Without peeking, each of you will write three sentences that are syntactically correct on your paper. Then, you'll each write three sentences that are syntactically *incorrect*. If you can't figure out how to do that, just write it how Yoda might say it: "A book about JavaScript programming, this is."

Now the fun begins: trade papers with your friend. You two will compete to see who can identify the syntactically correct and incorrect sentences the fastest! You can repeat this game over and over again.

# A Matter of Semantics

👤 1   🕐 10–15 minutes   ✗ Paper, pencil

## Activity Overview

This is very much like the Syntactically Correct activity, only this time, you're going to be thinking of semantics. Once you start running into runtime errors (get it?), you're going to want to debug your logic and structure. Figuring out these runtime, or semantic, errors is going to be kind of tough! That's why you need this activity.

## Instructions

To start off, find a friend. Without peeking, each of you will write three sentences that are semantically correct on your paper. Getting the semantics right is easy, like in this example: I enjoy cooking, my friends, and my dog. Then, you'll each write three sentences that are semantically incorrect. If you can't figure out how to do that, check out this example of bad semantics: I enjoy cooking my friends and my dog.

With that all done, trade papers with your friend. You two will compete to see who can identify the semantically correct and incorrect sentences the fastest! You can repeat this game over and over again.

# Variable Name Game

 2+   15–20 minutes    Sticky notes, pencil, a hat or bowl

## Activity Overview

Programming is rarely done alone. Nobody—from the young hotshot coder to the old veteran—works without a team. Teamwork makes the dream work, and it's very important to write clear and concise code for your teammates. One way to make your programs more understandable for your team is to name variables in a semantic way. What's that mean? For instance, if you're storing a value for the color red, just call your variable "red", or "redColor." Keep it simple! It's best to make your variable names as short as possible while still being descriptive.

# Instructions

Start off by having someone write down some common tasks and put them in a hat. Then, the first player should pull a task from the hat. Now, all of the players can try to write the shortest—but still descriptive—title for the result of the given task. Whoever has the most descriptive—but still short—variable name will win that round.

Check out some examples:
Task: "Wash the dishes" Result: "cleanDishes" (good), "theDishesAreClean" (not great)
Task: "Turn on the lights" Result: "lightsOn" (good), "theLightsAreTurnedOn" (not great)

# Data Structures

Programming is a pretty cool concept, as you already know. Programs are what make games, phones, and the entire internet work. But at their simplest, programs are just sets of instructions that operate on data. All the basics we went over in the last section are, well, basic. We won't get very far if all we're doing is simple arithmetic. All programming languages make use of data structures to help programmers deal with complex forms of data. Data structures are pretty important across all kinds of programming languages and are the building blocks of all applications. Most programming languages refer to these different data structures as types. Types are pretty easy to understand. They're kind of like nouns in English: a way of identifying or classifying a specific *type* of data, just like a noun classifies a certain person, place, or thing.

Most languages have what are called primitive types. These are the most basic data types that a language supports and are pretty common across different languages. Primitive types get a lot of screen time because they are responsible for a lot of the basic stuff that happens behind the scenes of your program. Some primitive types include:

- **Integers:** A data type that represents whole numbers. These numbers are written without a fractional component (no decimals!) and can be positive or negative.
  Examples: 1, -1, 2048, 0
- **Floats:** A data type that represents numbers that contain a fractional component. These can be positive or negative; also called floating point numbers.
  Examples: 1.0, -1.0003, 2048.24, 0.003
- **Strings:** A data type containing a "string" or sequence of characters. These characters can be letters, symbols, punctuation, or numerals.
  Examples: "cats.", "5 dogs", "The panda eats, shoots, and leaves"
- **Booleans:** A data type that can only be represented by either true or false. Also called logical data types, Booleans are used to control the logic and flow of your programs. Using Booleans also helps to add checks to your programs to make sure a task was executed properly.
  Examples: true, false.
- **Null:** A data type that points to a nonexistent place in memory. Using null types is a more advanced concept, but you can use them to your advantage to control the flow of your programs, among other things.
  Example: null.
- **Undefined:** A data type specific to JavaScript that represents a variable that is either undeclared or has been declared without any assignment. You will most likely encounter these "undefined" errors when you try to access a variable that's not there, either by spelling its name incorrectly or forgetting to ever declare it in the first place. Don't panic if you see an error message like this: "myVariable is not defined"! Look through your code and check to see if "myVariable" was ever assigned or if you just spelled it wrong.
  **myUndefined**; // a variable that is declared—but has nothing assigned to it—will be undefined

# Collections—Arrays and Dictionaries (Objects)

Okay, so primitive data types can be pretty tough to understand at first. But they're also pretty cool! They allow you to do all kinds of things in your programs. But what happens if you want to group some of them together and access them throughout your program? That's where collections come in.

One type of collection is called an array. Arrays are indexed collections of data that are made up of individual elements. An element is just a fancy term to describe the things that make up the array. You could think of an array as a roll of quarters, where each quarter is an element. Like a roll of quarters, each element goes in one after the other. To add elements to an array, you push them onto it. When you fill a roll of quarters, it works the same way. You start with the first one at the bottom of the roll, and push more quarters on top of it.

Putting quarters into a roll is all well and good, but what if you want to spend some of that money—how do you get quarters out of the roll? In the real world, you would pop a quarter off of the roll with your index finger and thumb. It's the same thing with an array (minus the finger and thumb): to get the last element of the array and remove it from the array, you pop it—that's all it takes!

Now, what about getting a quarter that's not at the beginning or end? This is where that "indexed" part comes in. When I say that an array is indexed, it just means that you can access each element by its numerical index in the array. Wait, what? That's some serious vocab to come out of nowhere. Let me explain.

Say you want to get the fifth quarter out of the roll. That would be accessing an element by its numerical index (in this case, five). Wow, that was easy! One thing to take into consideration, though, is that in most programming languages, arrays are zero indexed. That sounds scary, but all it means is that the first element in the array has an index of zero, rather than one.

So what does that look like? Well, in most languages (including JavaScript), you access array elements using square brackets:

- myArray[0] **// the first element**
- myArray[1] **// the second element**
- myArray[4] **// the fifth element**
- myArray[10] **// the eleventh element**

That's not too bad, is it? It may take a little bit of getting used to, but if you think of it as subtracting one from the index you want, it'll make things a lot easier. Keeping with this roll of quarters analogy, if I want the fifth quarter in the roll, its index would be [4]—which is 5 − 1.

But maybe you want to save, so you want to add quarters into your roll. In the same way, you can insert elements into the array at their index. Let's say I want to pull the fifth quarter out of the roll and put a new one in there. That would look something like this:

- myArray[4] = myNewValue;

You probably won't do a lot of accessing or setting individual elements like that because it makes for confusing and unpredictable code. Like, what if the array is sorted in a different way? The fifth quarter may not actually be the quarter you want— it may be the 23rd. Who knows!

That's why languages have maps, or dictionaries. A map is a type of collection—just like an array—but rather than accessing its elements by their index values, you use a key. A key is a label that is paired with, or "mapped to," a value. You may have heard of "key-value pairs" before—well, that's what a map is! Maps are much handier for storing data that you know needs to be accessed individually. This solves the problem of accessing a specific value in an indexed array, since you always know that "myKey" is going to get you the value paired with that key.

So what does accessing a value in a map look like? Unlike indexed arrays, you don't push or pop values from a map. Rather, you get them and set them based on their keys:

```
// to set
myMap['myKey'] = myValue
```

```
// to get
aValue = myMap['myKey']
```

It's worth noting that the same techniques you used to name your variables should apply when you're naming your keys. Keep them as short and descriptive as possible, and your code will make more sense to you and anyone who happens to look at it.

Maps and arrays can store all of the primitive types, and a lot of languages will also let you store other types, such as arrays, maps, functions, and objects (which we'll get into soon). We'll be working with arrays and maps a lot throughout the book, so this won't be the last you see of them!

# Do the Shuffle!

 3     15–20 minutes     Paper, pencil, two decks of playing cards

## Activity Overview

Indexes aren't just for books! To become a master modder, you're going to have to learn the ins and outs of accessing your code's arrays. This activity will help familiarize you with arrays and their terminology, such as indexes, pushing, and popping.

## Instructions

Start off by finding two friends and two sets of playing cards. Have your friends help you separate out the ace, 2, 3, 4, 5, 6, 7, 8, 9, and 10 cards from each deck—those are the only cards you'll need. The game starts with two separate decks and four separate draw piles. Each deck should be arranged face up in ascending order: ace on the bottom, 2, 3, 4, and 5 on top. Each draw pile should also be arranged face up in ascending order: 6 on the bottom, 7, 8, 9, and 10 on top.

To play the game, one person will tell the other two players what to do with their decks and card piles. Sound simple? Well, here's the twist: the player giving directions can use only array and index commands! You're probably thinking, "Hey, I'm not a computer!" That's what your cards are for. The instruction reader can give the following commands:

- pop (place the bottom card of the deck onto the top of the draw pile)
- push (add the top card from the draw pile onto the top of the deck)
- Retrieve X (present the card at index X—remember: An index always starts at 0!)
- Replace X (remove the card at index X and replace it with the top card from the draw pile)

The players receiving instructions will race against each other to be the first to do the right thing! Whoever gets done first will score a point—but be careful, because if one player gets it wrong, the other player scores a point automatically. If both players get it wrong, the instruction reader gets a point!

After giving ten instructions, it's time to change things up. Both sets of cards should rotate clockwise to the next player. Since there are only two sets, that means there will be a new instruction reader. Repeat the game until everyone has had a chance to read instructions, then count up everyone's score! Who won?

# Taking Inventory

 1    10–30 minutes    Paper, pencil

## Activity Overview

A lot of games, including *Minecraft*, require that the player maintain an inventory of items. This is the perfect chance to implement a map to help you organize those items!

## Instructions

If you have your computer handy, start up *Minecraft* and take a look at your inventory. Go through each item and think of what you'd name a key for it. How would you organize your inventory in a map? How would you keep it consistent if you wanted to share it with a friend? You've got to think about this stuff while you code! You may also need to think about using a combination of data structures in your inventory. For instance, maybe you have several concrete blocks at your disposal, so you would likely want to store those in an array within your inventory map. Try to plot the map out in any way that's clear to you. Sometimes it helps to draw arrows:

myInventory --> myBlocks **// map** --> concrete --> 25 **// array**
                                      marble ----> 10 **// array**
                                      wood ----> 13 **// array**

# Control Flow

Even after all these pages of learning, any code you write is going to be pretty simple. You know how to do some basic arithmetic, assign some variables, and store some data in some structures. That's all pretty cool stuff, but where programs really start to get interesting is in their logic. The practice of adding logic to your programs is called control flow. That means that you're adding code to control the flow of your program—think of it as being kind of like a "choose your own adventure" novel. If a user tries to do one thing, the program will flow in a specific way. Hopefully this gives them their desired result—or maybe it drops them in a den of lions. Who knows!

The main tool at your disposal for control flow is the IF statement. This is the holy grail of all programming languages—once you can master this, you can do anything. Well, almost. An IF statement is deceptively simple, and works pretty much in the following manner:

```
if (some condition) {
        Do this
} else {
        Do that
}
```

Not too bad for being one of your most powerful tools, right? So, the condition referenced in that statement could be a lot of things: it could compare the value of one variable to another; it could check to see if a value exists; it could check to see if one number is larger than another, etc. It's these conditions that hold the true power of the IF statement, and thankfully you already know some of them from the previous sections!

The conditions in IF statements use a combination of what are called comparison operators and logical operators. Like the name suggests, a comparison operator is used to compare two values. Here are some examples of comparison operators:

- == (compares if two values are equal)
- Example: (1 == 1) **// true**
  - === (compares if two values are equal and have the same type—also known as "strict equal")
- Example: (1 === "1") **// false**
  - != (comparison to see if two values are not equal; known as "not equal")
- Example: (2 != 1) **// true**
  - !== (comparison to see if two values are either not equal, or not of the same type. Known as "strict not equal")
- Examples: ('1' !== 1) **// true** ; (1 !== 1) **// false**
  - > (comparison to see if the left operand is greater than the right)
- Example: (2 > 1) **// true**
  - < (comparison to see if the left operand is less than the right)
- Example: (2 < 1) **// false**
  - >= (comparison to see if the left operand is greater than or equal to the right)
- Example: (2 >= 2) **// true**
  - <= (comparison to see if the left operand is less than or equal to the right)
- Example: (1 <= 2) **// true**

There are only a handful of logical operators to use with the conditional operators. These are especially useful for shorthand, or for chaining conditions. Here are some logical operators:

- && (the "and" operator checks if two conditions are met)
  - Example: (2 > 1 && 1 !== '1') **// true**
- || (the "or" operator checks to see if at least one of the conditions is met)
  - Example: myOne = 1
  - (myOne === 1 || myOne < 0) **// true because the first condition was met**
- ! (a nice shorthand operator to check if a value is true; particularly useful for checking if variables are set or not)
  - Examples: myOne; **// myOne never assigned**
    - (!myOne) **// true**
    - myTrue = true;
    - (!myTrue) **// false**

Now that you know what IF statements are all about, it's time to learn how to use them! Remember, the most basic IF statement looks something like this:

```
if (some condition) {
        // do something
} else {
        // do something else
}
```

Well, what if you need to combine multiple conditions? Thankfully, because of a concept called scoping, IF statements can be nested:

```
if (some condition) {
// this IF statement is nested in the scope of the above IF statement
        if (some other condition) {
```

```
        // do something here
} else {
        // do something different
}
} else {
    // do something else
}
```

There is no limit to how deeply you can nest IF statements, but be warned: the greater the depth, the greater the complexity. And the greater the complexity, the more difficult it is to read! Luckily, most languages (including JavaScript) have more efficient ways of establishing control flow.

For instance, JavaScript has something called an ELSE-IF statement, which allows you to chain conditions. In other words, you're not stuck with the simple "if-then-else" pattern:

```
if (some condition){
        // do something
} else if (another condition){
        // do something
} else {
        // do the last thing
}
```

You can string together multiple ELSE-IF statements, as long as the first statement is IF and the last statement is ELSE. But that can get kind of sloppy, too! Some languages, JavaScript included, can make use of something called a switch statement, which is useful when you have a block of code with lots of conditions, or clauses. The switch statement can be kind of confusing, so a concrete example will work best.

Let's say you're writing a mod that allows a user to launch blocks in *Minecraft*. Because the blocks are made from different materials, they'll have different physical behaviors when you launch them. In a switch statement, you could take the block's type as an expression and assign different behavior based on this material type:

```
// assume the block and blockType variables are being set
somewhere else in the program.
// the switch statement takes the blockType variable as an argument
and the block variable is in the scope of that statement, so we still
have access to it.
switch(blockType) {
    case 'rubber':
    // code to make the block bouncy
    break;
    case 'glass':
    // code to make the block shatter
    break;
    case 'wood':
    // code to make the block splinter
    break;default:
    // set default behavior if the type is none of the above
}
```

Alright, so there's a lot going on in that code example. As I mentioned, switch(blockType) takes the block's type as the expression in question. All of the different "cases" are like IF statements. They actually function like this:

```
if (blockType === 'rubber') {
        // code to make the block bouncy
} else if (blockType === 'glass') {
        // code to make the block shatter
} else if (blockType === 'wood') {
        // code to make the block splinter

} else {
    // set default behavior if the type is none of the above
```

```
}
```

This code is a lot more complicated! You can see where using a switch is especially useful if you have a lot of cases. But if you're really attached to chaining IF and ELSE-IF statements, be my guest. Both of the previous examples are semantically correct. The "right" choice is the one you—and your programming partners—decide works best for you.

All of those break statements that you see at the end of the cases ensure that our program is properly exiting out of the resulting code block for each case. You'll learn more about breaks when we get to the next section on looping and iteration. The only other thing that may look strange to you is the default clause at the end of the switch. This is like the final "else" in an IF statement—if the expression doesn't match any of the conditions, the program defaults to, well, the default.

# Twenty Questions

 2    20–40 minutes   ✖ Sticky notes, pencil

## Activity Overview

This activity should remind you of the game Twenty Questions, where one player (the answerer) comes up with an object and tries to stump the other players. The other players have twenty chances (questions) to guess the object. In this case, the questioners have to use logical and conditional operators in their questions!

## Instructions

Pick one player as the answerer to start. Once that person has thought up some object, each player needs to write down his or her questions in the form of conditional statements. For instance, if you're trying to guess the color of the object, you would write "color == red." Then, the answerer must return Boolean results (true or false).

Rotate through each questioner until someone either guesses the correct answer or the twenty questions are all used up. If someone guesses the correct answer, that person becomes the answerer for the next round. If the questioners are stumped, the answerer gets to go again in the next round. Go for as many rounds as you want—the answerer with the most "stumps" wins!

# Choose Your Own Adventure

 1     20–30 minutes     Paper, pencil

## Activity Overview

Get ready to adventure! In this activity, you'll be using your newfound IF and switch statement skills to create a flow diagram to make a simple choose-your-own-adventure-scenario. If you haven't heard of them, choose-your-own-adventure novels were books that gave readers scenarios that required their input. Based on the reader's choice, they would turn to a given page in the book that advanced the story.

## Instructions

Using a piece of paper, draw out your own choose-your-own-adventure scenario. This can be in the form of a flow diagram, a map, or whatever design you feel comfortable with. Start off with a basic idea—who's the character? Where do they live? What do they look like? From there, build "branches" and multiple pathways through your story. Ultimately, your goal is to have a single starting point that can lead off in a bunch of different directions.

If you don't have any ideas, here's a prompt for you: create a scenario where the reader is stuck in a dungeon and needs to find his or her way out.

# Looping and Iteration

By now, I bet you have a pretty good grasp on how you can logically structure your programs. Another big part of programming (and what makes programs so exciting!) is the concept of iteration. Iteration gives us the ability to repeat things, or create loops. We can iterate over collections, like arrays, repeat tasks for a set duration, and even run a loop until the end of time! A loop is kind of like an IF statement that repeats for a certain amount of time. That might sound confusing, but it's really not.

A loop takes a condition and executes it a set number of times based on that condition. In JavaScript, and in many other languages, there are two types of loops. The first is called a FOR loop, and is probably the one you see the most. A FOR loop takes a condition and runs until that condition is met. In plain English, you could describe a FOR loop like this:

> Come up with a condition and do something. When you're done doing something, check to see if the condition is true. If it still isn't true, do something again. Repeat until the condition is true

Pretty straightforward, right? The other type is a while loop, and it runs while a condition is met. It goes something like this:

> Come up with a condition and do something. When you're done doing something, check to see if the condition is false. If it still isn't false, do something again. Repeat until the condition is false

You may think, "hmm, there's not much difference between those." When we get to chapter two and start writing some code, you'll notice that there's a big difference! Pretty much anything you can do with a FOR loop, you can also do with a while loop. The big difference is that a FOR loop has a set beginning and end, and it involves incrementation.

When we increment something, it just means that we're adding a number to it. Take a set of stairs, for example. When we start, we're at step zero. Every step we take, we increment our step count by one. Our "stair-climbing loop" is finished when we reach the top of the stairs. The FOR loop version of our exciting stair example would be something like this:

> **Our first step is step zero, so our step count is zero. There are ten steps. If our step count is less than ten, we take a step. We keep going up one step until our step count is ten and we've reached the top of the stairs.**

A FOR loop is particularly useful for counting and has incrementation built in. A while loop is easier to write, but you have to handle the incrementation yourself if you need to do any sort of counting. You would use a while loop to iterate for a duration you don't know the end of. For example: listening for a user input. Let's look at a more interesting (and tasty) example.

We have a pizza, and it's got a bunch of mushrooms on it. We don't like them and we want to take them off and feed them to our dog. A FOR loop version would look something like this:

> **Our mushroom count is zero. There are eight mushrooms on our slice of pizza. We take one mushroom off of the pizza and give it to our dog. If our mushroom count is less than eight, we take one mushroom off at a time and give it to our dog until there are zero mushrooms left.**

A while loop (without us writing incrementation on our own) looks something like this:

> Our pizza has some mushrooms on it. We take a mushroom off and give it to our dog. We check to see if it still has mushrooms. We take another one off and give it to our dog. We keep doing this until there are no mushrooms left.

We can simplify our pizza loops like this:

- FOR loop: For every mushroom on the pizza, take one mushroom off until there are no mushrooms left.
- While loop: While there are mushrooms on the pizza, take a mushroom off.

# The Best Activity in the Book

 1     10–15 minutes     Bag of candy or a snack that has multiple pieces

## Activity Overview

It's tough to understand abstract concepts like FOR and while loops, but it's easier when you're dealing with real-world things—especially if these real-world things are edible! Based on the prompts in this activity, you'll have to guess if the way you're eating your snacks is a while loop or a FOR loop. If you get full, you can still do the activity without eating—or come back to it when you want dessert!

## Instructions

Got your candy ready? With the following prompts, guess which are while loops and which are FOR loops. In some cases, the prompts may have both!

1. Pick up three pieces of your snack and put them in your right hand. Eat the pieces until there are none left.
2. Eat one piece of your snack. Then another. Then another. Then another. Then another. Then another.
3. Eat two more pieces, one at a time.
4. Eat one piece every five seconds until thirty seconds have passed.
5. Put a piece of your snack on the table every ten seconds until a minute has passed. Eat each piece one by one.
6. Eat everything until there is nothing left.

Iteration is something you're going to be doing a lot of as you continue to learn how to program. Once we get to the next section and we start iterating over real collections (like your *Minecraft* inventory), it should make a lot of sense. Trust me— even if you're a little lost now, you'll get lots of practice.

Another concept we need to get through before we start writing some code is the idea of a function. Functions are hugely important programming constructs, and they're relatively straightforward to understand. I like to think of functions as a way of packaging up useful code that we've written, with the intention of reusing it. As we write our programs and they grow increasingly more complicated, we should rely on functions to help us keep everything clean and organized. A function is a named block of code that we can call within our program or in other programs that we write.

Take our pizza exercise: You don't want to have to write out the same instructions for every piece of pizza requiring mushroom removal, especially if you're doing the same thing every time! There is a popular programming principle known as DRY: don't repeat yourself. It makes a lot more sense for us to create a function called "removeMushrooms" than to keep rewriting the same code over and over again. Repeating code over and over again would be known as a WET solution to our problem (we enjoy typing).

A function has three key components. It needs a name (i.e., removeMushrooms), it has parameters or arguments (variables that we do something with in the function), and it may or may not have a return value, which is what the function "gives back," or returns, when it's done.

Let's break down our removeMushrooms example. We already have a name! Easy. Now we can think about what arguments we need to "pass" into the function. Well, we'll need our slice of mushroom pizza, and we'll need the dog that we're going to feed the mushrooms to. Our function could then return the slice of pizza with mushrooms removed. Let's try this out on some more examples!

# Looping

 1    10–15 minutes    Paper, pencil

## Activity Overview

I hope you aren't sick of FOR and while loops yet because this activity is really going to test your skills. You'll have to look at some scenarios and come up with your very own looping strategy.

## Instructions

Check out the following scenarios. For each one, write a FOR loop and while loop version of how you'd solve the problem.

1.  You have a newspaper route and you have to deliver twenty papers to twenty houses.
2.  When you get to the first house, you have to walk up fourteen steps to get to the door.
3.  When you go to drop off the paper, five bees come buzzing at you and you have to swat them with the paper.

4. After you take out the bees, you notice that you ripped your pants. You have to run home three blocks to change them.
5. When you get home, you realize that you don't have any pants that go with your shirt (fashion is very important). You go through six drawers of clothes until you find some cool pants.

# What's the Function?

 1    10–15 minutes    Paper, pencil

## Activity Overview

Understanding how to use functions in your programs is going to make your life so much easier—trust me. In this activity, you're going to get some good practice using real-life examples.

## Instructions

Try to come up with a function for each of the following tasks. Remember: each function should have a name, some arguments, and depending on the situation, a return value.

1. You're having a snowball fight with your friends. You need to make a snowball that is ready to throw.
2. You pop a tire on your bike. You need to patch the tire and fill it with air.
3. You have some change and you need $1.25 for a soda. You need to count the change and put the rest back in your pocket.
4. You want to play *Minecraft* but you need to log in. What information do you need?
5. There are zombies outside your house and you need to barricade your door (at least one of these should be interesting, right?)

# What's the Function? The Sequel

 1   10–15 minutes   Paper, pencil

## Activity Overview

Okay, hotshot—you think that coming up with functions is pretty easy, don't you? Well, now you can try to work backward. A big part of programming with others is writing clear, concise code with lots of documentation. In addition to documentation, the function names and arguments should be very clear so others know how to use them. Code doesn't help anyone if no one can understand it!

## Instructions

Based on the functions below, try to figure out what they do. They all have pretty vague names and arguments. Come up with some better ones!

1.  walk(animal, leash, park)
2.  toss(wrapper, can)
3.  build(hammer, nails, tree, plan)
4.  dig(map, location)

Ah, functions. They'll save you a ton of time and are absolutely necessary and central to writing larger programs—especially in JavaScript. Once we get rolling here, you'll also learn about some really cool things you can do with functions and why JavaScript is considered a functional language, which is what is know as a programming paradigm. But let's not get too intense just yet!

JavaScript is a language that supports many programming paradigms. What this means for us is that the JavaScript interpreter doesn't care about how we write our programs. It cares only that they're syntactically correct. How we design our programs is completely up to us, but there are certain established patterns we can follow that will not only keep our programs organized, but will make them easier for others to read and understand.

Java, the language that *Minecraft* is built in, follows a paradigm known as object-oriented programming. JavaScript also supports object-oriented programming out of the box, and we will be using it throughout the book. The biggest thing you'll need to know about object orientation is that it works on the principles of classes and objects.

Classes represent real-world things in an abstract way. Think about blocks in *Minecraft*. While there are many different types of blocks, they all have similar characteristics that make them blocks as opposed to, say, trees. A class is kind of like a mold that we can use to make a bunch of blocks from. Objects are the instances, or individual blocks, that are produced from the mold. Each individual block has its own characteristics, or properties, that describe it. It also has its own functions—or methods—that define its behavior.

That's a pretty technical way of looking at these terms, though. Let's simplify! We can think of classes as nouns, properties as adjectives, and methods as verbs. If we had a class called Block, some of its properties could include its width, height, depth, and type of material—all things that can help us to describe it. We could also come up with some methods that define the block's behavior or manipulate it in a certain way.

To recap, a property contains information about an aspect of an object, while a method does something with the object. The class is what contains these properties and methods.

# Getting Classy

 1    10–15 minutes    Paper, pencil

## Activity Overview

If you want to work on larger programs, you're going to need to know how to deal with classes. Structuring your classes helps you keep everything organized. It also allows you to reuse a lot of code between programs! The first step of organizing your classes is naming them.

## Instructions

Given the groupings of properties and methods below, come up with a class name for each of them. For example: .

1. type, hasTail, scratch, purr
2. drive, reverse, numberOfDoors, numberOfWheels
3. flavor, isDiet, hasCaffeine, volume, isCan
4. toppings, sauce, crustType
5. flavor, toppings, hasCone
6. brand, isWaterproof, type, color, size, laceColor
7. manufacturer, storageSize, screenSize, operatingSystem
8. volume, radius, circumference, weight, isRegulationSize, airLevel
9. title, numberOfPages, chapters

So what would our simple Block class look like? Well, like I mentioned before, it's going to have some properties that it'll share with all blocks. It's going to have a width, a height, and a depth. The block should also have some sort of property specifying what type of material it's made of, such as wood, stone, or dirt. Maybe we also want to give it a scale property so we can grow it or shrink it. When we instantiate (which is just a fancy word for creating an instance of the block), we can set all of these properties in what's called a constructor. A constructor is a special type of function that takes a set of arguments and returns a new object with some of its properties already set. You can also set an object's properties after it has been instantiated. Remember, properties are just information about the object that help us figure out what class it's in—they are variables that store useful information about the individual object.

# Name Game

 2     20–25 minutes     Sticky notes, pencil

## Activity Overview

This activity is based on a classic game where players are given the names of famous people. A name is stuck to each player's forehead where he or she can't see it. The players try to guess who they are by asking each other questions about whose name is stuck on their foreheads. You're going to be doing that—but instead of famous people, you're going to use classes.

## Instructions

In this case, the players are given names of classes, like Cat, Car, Pizza, or Ice Cream. They must ask about their properties in order to get an answer. This will help to get you to think about what properties are necessary in order for a class to accurately portray the real-world object it's supposed to represent.

Start off by having each player write the name of a class on a sticky note. This can be anything he or she wants! As long as it's a noun, it's fair game. Then, each player will put his or her sticky note on someone else's forehead—and no peeking! Everybody has to ask each other about the properties of each other's given classes. If a player guesses the class correctly, he or she takes the name off his or her forehead. The first one to guess correctly wins the round!

Methods are just functions that are part of a given class. They are tied to the individual object and often play with its properties or produce some sort of result based on them. For instance, our block may have a method to calculate its surface area or volume. It may also have a method to trigger some sort of effect when it collides with a player. Let's just say our block shrinks when a player collides with it—we could come up with an onCollide method that then alters the block's scale property and makes it smaller.

# A Method to the Madness

 2+  ⏱ 20–30 minutes   Sticky notes, index cards, hat or bowl, paper, pencil

## Activity Overview

One thing you're going to get really good at is using functions and methods to operate on—and change—data structures. Why? Because you're going to be doing it a lot! This is known as mutability, meaning that a piece of data can be mutated, or changed.

Functions and methods often take a piece of data as an input and return the data as an output, either as a copy or as the newly modified original. You're going to practice this with some random drawing.

## Instructions

Start off by taking your index cards and writing down one type of "drawing method" on each one. This "method" could be something like "draw a hat" or "fill in half with green." Be creative!

One of the players should then draw something cool on a piece of paper. Take turns pulling the "tasks" from the hat, and modify the image based on the task. It'll probably look pretty weird when you're done. Maybe one of you will become the next Picasso!

# Tying It All Together

 1     10–15 minutes     Paper, pencil

## Activity Overview

A very common software development practice is to draw out or model your classes. This allows for developers to not only think about what methods and properties a class needs, but also how they relate to and interact with other classes. Make sure you make a good model! It'll come up again in chapter three.

## Instructions

Before you can do anything, you need to come up with what kind of class you'd create. Got it? Now, grab a piece of paper and write down all of the methods and properties for that class. Later on in the book, you'll be writing a class that creates random dungeons and fills them with mobs and loot. If you want, you can try to write out some of the inner workings of that class. Or you could start simple—maybe you want to explore the Block class we've been talking about or maybe something completely different!

Phew, we went through a lot in this chapter, didn't we? The good news is that now you've got some fundamental ideas down. I think you're ready to dive right into some programming! In the next chapter, we're going to set up SpigotMC (the *Minecraft* server ScriptCraft runs on) and get ScriptCraft up and running. We'll be practicing all of the stuff we talked about here as well as learning some new techniques. Fire up that computer of yours and let's get started!

# Chapter Two

# INTRODUCTION TO JAVASCRIPT AND SCRIPTCRAFT

Congratulations, you made it through all of the theory! Throughout this section, we'll be exploring everything you learned in chapter one in a concrete way. We'll start by getting ScriptCraft and SpigotMC up and running, which will teach us how to download software and run it from the command line. From there, we'll actually be able to start executing code right in *Minecraft*—the really exciting stuff. Pretty soon, we'll be able to see just how powerful programming can be! Want to automatically populate your inventory? Done! Want to build structures and place blocks? Done! Want to create your own plugin and custom items? Done! Want to add a bunch of stuff to the world and blow it all up? Done and done! There's nothing cooler than being able to see our progress in real time. The future is now!

Each activity in this chapter will require a computer, a copy of *Minecraft: Java Edition*, and the SpigotMC Server with ScriptCraft installed unless otherwise noted.

# Installing SpigotMC

 1    **20–30 minutes**

## Activity Overview

SpigotMC is the popular *Minecraft* mod server that ScriptCraft runs on. You're going to want to get familiar with installing programs to work with *Minecraft*, and this activity is here to help! You're also going to get a very basic introduction to using a command line interface (CLI).

## Instructions

Note: if you get stuck, you can also consult the official Scriptcraft documentation at https://github.com/walterhiggins/ScriptCraft.

1. Download the SpigotMC build tools, which can be found here: https://hub.spigotmc.org/jenkins/job/BuildTools /lastSuccessfulBuild/artifact/target/BuildTools.jar. By running these build tools, we're actually going to build and install the SpigotMC *Minecraft* Server.

2. Because SpigotMC runs on Java, you'll also need to download and install the Java Development Kit (JDK). You can download the installer for the appropriate operating system here: http://www.oracle.com/technetwork/java/javase/downloads /jdk8-downloads-2133151.html. Follow the instructions to complete the JDK installation.

3. Now, create a directory to put your SpigotMC build in. This can be anywhere, but I recommend you don't put it on your desktop—put it somewhere that's easy for you to find or remember. While this isn't necessary, I like to create a folder off of my home directory called Applications, where I put all of the software that I either create or modify. Let's

assume from now on everything we do is going to be in this Applications directory.

- The home directory on a Mac is /Users/yourusername
- On Windows, it's C:\Users\yourusername

Create an Applications folder in your home directory, and in that Applications folder, create another one called spigotmc.

4. Copy the SpigotMC BuildTools.jar file to your spigotmc directory.

5. Now, open up a command line terminal. On a Mac, this is an application called Terminal. On Windows, you can open either a PowerShell or Command Prompt.

6. The terminal or command prompt should open in your home directory. You need to cd or "change directories" to get to your home/Applications/spigotmc directory.

- Simply type *cd spigotmc* and you should find yourself there!

7. From your spigotmc directory, type *java -jar BuildTools.jar*. This command will begin to compile SpigotMC for you. Once the installation has completed, you should get a message along the lines of, "Success! Everything compiled successfully."

8. Once everything has been compiled, you can get a list of all of the files in the spigotmc directory by typing "ls" on a Mac or "dir" on Windows. You should see a file called spigot-[version number will change].jar. To start up the server, all you have to do is type *java-jar spigot-[version number].jar*.

9. You probably got an error saying you have to agree to the EULA (end user license agreement). Don't worry, this is normal! To agree, you just have to open up the file in a text editor (TextEdit on a Mac or Notepad on Windows) or your favorite IDE (more on that later). Now, look for the line *"eula=false"* and change it to *"eula=true"* and save the file.

10. Now, you should be able to run that same line again: *java-jar spigot-[version number].jar* to start the server.

11. The server will step through some configurations, and once that's done, you should receive a message telling you that the configuration is done. Congratulations! You installed SpigotMC. To stop the server, just type *stop* at the server prompt to safely shut it down.

# Installing ScriptCraft

 1   **20–30 minutes**

## Activity Overview

Now that you've installed SpigotMC, you must be itching to get programming! And how do you do that? You're going to go ahead and install ScriptCraft!

## Instructions

1. Download the most up-to-date ScriptCraft .jar file from: https://scriptcraftjs.org/download/latest.

2. Once you've downloaded the jar file, copy it to the plugins folder in your spigotmc directory. Plugins are a way of extending a software application—kind of like mods for development! All of the SpigotMC plugins you use will go in this folder and will automatically be loaded at runtime.

3. Start up your SpigotMC server by typing *java -jar spigot-[version number].jar*. Everything should start up like it did before, and you should be prompted with a "Done" message.

4.  Okay! Let's test to see if ScriptCraft is working. At the server prompt, try this:

    js console.log("hello world!");

    Pretty cool, right? The first step on your coding journey is complete!

One of the many great things about ScriptCraft is that it uses the JVM's (Java Virtual Machine) native JavaScript engine—called Nashorn—to interpret all of the code you write on the fly. What you just did here was execute one of JavaScript's core functions, which logs messages to the console. You have access to all of the core JavaScript functions, which you'll soon discover!

# Connecting to a Server

 1    10–20 minutes

## Activity Overview

Once we've got our server up and running, it would be pretty nice if we could communicate with it in the game. Otherwise, how are you going to get all your code to work? In this activity, you'll actually connect to the server and execute some simple JavaScript code from the chat terminal!

## Instructions

1.  Start up your SpigotMC server with the "golden command": *java -jar spigot-[version number].jar*

2. Open *Minecraft* and select multiplayer. From there, click Add Server. You'll be met with a prompt to edit the server info. For the server name, you can call it whatever you want. For the server address, type in *localhost*. Once you've done this, just click Done. This means that we're running the server locally, and that it's not broadcasting out to the world!

3. You should now be able to see your server in the list of servers. Click on it, and select Join Server.

4. You should now find yourself in a new *Minecraft* game. Yes! You should also be greeted with a message that welcomes you to ScriptCraft.

5. To type a command, you can open the chat terminal by pressing "t" or typing "/." Now, to enter JavaScript code, you need to make sure your commands are prefixed with a "/js" or else they'll get treated like regular chat messages. Try something like this:
/js 2+2

6.  No! It most likely didn't work, did it? You probably got some message about how you don't have permissions to evaluate blah blah blah. Well, that's because ScriptCraft requires that you have operator permissions on the server in order to execute JavaScript code. An operator (op) is a role that is granted all permissions on the server. To make yourself an op (and why would you not want to?!), type 'op [username]' at the server prompt. Once that's done, now you should be able to run JavaScript code from the chat prompt. Try to run that first method we ran on the server earlier:

console.log("hello, world!")

You should see the message show up on the server—nice!

```
[10:28:23 INFO]: Mob Spawn Range: 4
[10:28:23 INFO]: View Distance: 10
[10:28:23 INFO]: Nerfing mobs spawned from spawners: false
[10:28:23 INFO]: Cactus Growth Modifier: 100%
[10:28:23 INFO]: Cane Growth Modifier: 100%
[10:28:23 INFO]: Melon Growth Modifier: 100%
[10:28:23 INFO]: Mushroom Growth Modifier: 100%
[10:28:23 INFO]: Pumpkin Growth Modifier: 100%
[10:28:23 INFO]: Sapling Growth Modifier: 100%
[10:28:23 INFO]: Wheat Growth Modifier: 100%
[10:28:23 INFO]: NetherWart Growth Modifier: 100%
[10:28:23 INFO]: Vine Growth Modifier: 100%
[10:28:23 INFO]: Cocoa Growth Modifier: 100%
[10:28:23 INFO]: Entity Activation Range: An 32 / Mo 32 / Mi 16
[10:28:23 INFO]: Entity Tracking Range: Pl 48 / An 48 / Mo 48 / Mi 32 / Other 64
[10:28:23 INFO]: Hopper Transfer: 8 Hopper Check: 1 Hopper Amount: 1
[10:28:23 INFO]: Random Lighting Updates: false
[10:28:23 INFO]: Structure Info Saving: true
[10:28:23 INFO]: Custom Map Seeds:  Village: 10387312 Feature: 14357617 Monument: 10387313 Slime: 987234911
[10:28:23 INFO]: Max TNT Explosions: 100
[10:28:23 INFO]: Tile Max Tick Time: 50ms Entity max Tick Time: 50ms
[10:28:23 INFO]: Allow Zombie Pigmen to spawn from portal blocks: true
[10:28:23 INFO]: Arrow Despawn Rate: 1200
[10:28:23 INFO]: Preparing start region for level 0 (Seed: -625897789037736128)
[10:28:24 INFO]: Preparing spawn area: 27%
[10:28:24 INFO]: Preparing start region for level 1 (Seed: 8399995367636833795)
[10:28:25 INFO]: Preparing spawn area: 81%
[10:28:25 INFO]: Preparing start region for level 2 (Seed: 8399995367636833795)
[10:28:26 INFO]: [ScriptCraftEvent] Enabling ScriptCraftEvent v1.0.0
[10:28:26 INFO]: [scriptcraft] Enabling scriptcraft v3.2.1-2016-12-23
[10:28:28 WARN]: [scriptcraft] cow-clicker minigame is not yet supported in CanaryMod and Craftbukkit
[10:28:30 INFO]: Server permissions file permissions.yml is empty, ignoring it
[10:28:30 INFO]: Done (8.256s)! For help, type "help" or "?"
[10:28:30 INFO]: [scriptcraft] js-patch setTimeout() test complete
>|
```

# Taking Some Shortcuts

 1    10–15 minutes

## Activity Overview

It's kind of annoying that we have to go into the SpigotMC directory and type that Java command every time we want to start the server. Let's make a desktop shortcut to fire up the server and save us a few steps! Your schedule will thank me later.

## Instructions

### On OSX

1. Open up your text editor and create a new file. Go to Format→ Make Plain Text. Save the file to your desktop as start-spigotmc.command

2. Add the following line: #!/bin/bash. That command is going to tell your operating system to execute this script in the bash shell.

3. Add a command to change directories into your spigotmc directory: cd /path/to/your/spigotmc (where the path is your local path to the spigotmc folder)

4. Add two ampersands after the path you just typed (&&) followed by the java command we've been using: java -jar spigot-1.12.2.jar

5. Your file should now look like this:
   *#!/bin/bash*
   *cd /Users/[your name]/Applications/spigotmc/ && java -jar spigot-[your spigotmc version].jar*

6. Great! Now this is the part where it gets tricky—but you'll only have to do it once. Open up the terminal and cd into the directory that holds your start-spigotmc.command file. In my case: cd /Users/joshr/Desktop.

7. Now you have to change the permissions on the file, which means that you can set which users can read, write, or execute (run) the file. You're going to use a tool called chmod to do that. All you have to do is type in this command:
   *chmod u+x start-spigotmc.command*
   That looks like a huge hassle, but all it's doing is telling the operating system that you want to set permissions to allow the user (u) to execute (+x) the start-spigotmc.command file.

8. You should be all set now. Double-click on the file and watch as your terminal magically opens up and starts your server!

## On Windows

1. Open up a text editor, like Notepad. Create a new file and go to save it (*File→ save*). At the bottom of the window, select "Save as Type" to "all files" and name the file start-spigotmc.cmd.

2. Now, in the file, type *cd C:\{the path to your spigotmc folder}*. In my case, it would be cd C:\Users\joshr\Applications\spigotmc.

3. On the next line, all you have to do is type the Java command

we used to start up the SpigotMC server:
*java -jar spigot-{your spigotmc version}.jar*
4. Now you should be able to double-click the file on your desktop and start up the server. Easy!

It's worth noting that all of the stuff we did in this section is common for setting up and running most of the software you'll write as you move on from this book. There is always some sort of build system, libraries, or server configuration that you'll need to take into account and set up. It's always helpful to practice your command line skills if you want to continue to explore programming! Even though you've now got the skills to set yourself up, there are tools out there that can help you set up your development environment—you don't always have to do it from scratch. Other programmers who've experienced this stuff firsthand are out there to help, and the community of developers on sites like Stack Overflow (https://stackoverflow.com) is ready to help you fix all your programming problems.

## The Basics

Now that everything is up and running—finally—we can start some actual programming! We're going to look back at the primitive types that we were talking about in chapter one. We're going to start with another "hello world" program, and from there we'll get into variables—one of the most important concepts in any programming language. From variables, it's on to numbers, strings, Booleans, and all of the other primitives. Hope you're excited!

JavaScript has a lot of support for its primitive types, and that's good news. We'll be able to explore the many different functions it has for dealing with them. You'll be able to practice with these methods, and you'll use them to help creatively solve problems in your larger programs. You'll also learn about some nitty-gritty programmer stuff, like comments and cases, which will help you create more uniform, understandable code in the future. Alright, enough with the talk—let's get down to business!

# Hello World: The Sequel

 1  5–10 minutes

## Activity Overview

Now that you've got your fancy shortcut to start up SpigotMC, fire up *Minecraft* and get that server running. From here on in, we're going to be writing JavaScript! We're going to go back to step six of the Connecting to a Server activity. What you basically did there was your first "hello world" program. You're going to do another one here, and check out the different types of logging available to you.

## Instructions

Join your server and open up your command prompt with the "/" key. First, you're going to repeat what you did in Connecting to a Server and type (remember—you have to add "js" first):

console.log('hello, world!');

Wait, where did it go? Did anything happen? Take a look into your terminal / command prompt window and you should see "hello, world" in your server output. Cool, but why didn't it show up on the screen? Technically, the console.log() method does not print messages to the screen. In browsers, it prints messages to the developer console, while in NodeJS, it prints messages out to the terminal. This is a tool that you will use for debugging your programs—and pretty much nothing else. Still, it's very handy.

Alright, but what if we want to actually print messages out to the screen so that other players can see them—like status updates or something? If we were writing JavaScript in the browser, we would have to create HTML elements to display the messages. Luckily, ScriptCraft has a function that prints content to the in-game console. Try this:

```
echo(self, 'hello, world');
```

Pretty neat! You'll be doing a lot with that "self" variable in later activities, so keep it in the back of your mind.

Finally, if you've had some experience with web programming, there is also an alias for the echo function called alert. In the browser, the JavaScript alert function displays an alert window on your screen. Try to see what it does here (hint: just replace echo with alert).

# Commenting for Clarity

 1  10–15 minutes

## Activity Overview

Picture this: You're writing some code. It makes a lot of sense to you, but your friend just doesn't get it. How can you help him? The answer is simple: comments! Comments are blocks of code that are ignored by the compiler, so they're never run. They can help to make your code clearer and can even be used to generate documentation. You're going to take a look at how to make single-line and multi-line comments in JavaScript.

## Instructions

To make a single-line comment in JavaScript, you use "//"

**// this is a single-line comment**

To make multi-line comments, you use "/*" to open the comment, and "*/" to close it:

/* This is a multi-
line comment */

It's worth noting that a single-line comment will treat a whole line as a comment, so if you only need to comment on a section of an otherwise perfect line, you'll have to use a multi-line comment. Check it out:

console.log("Hello " + //"World"); OH NO! This whole line is a comment!
console.log("Hello " + /* "World" */ "Steve");
>> "Hello Steve"

Okay, let's see if you're up for this task: I fell asleep working on this book and my cat stepped all over the keyboard. Typical. Can you find all of the places where he "made his contribution" and comment them out? Try to figure out where you need to make multi-line or single-line comments.

What if we're writing dfdfddddfd our code and we want to leave sdasw messages fsddor ourselves or eeffvv others? Here we'll take a look dfda at how to make single-line and vvddqq mulqqdti-line comments in aaaaaaaaaaaaasddddddddddssssssssdddddddddddddddsssdddddd sssdddddsd JavaScript. weeacgwComments are qqqwblocks of code that arc e ignored by the co awmpiler, so they're nggeever run. They can help to weesmake your code clearer, and can even bwwe used to generate documentatioqwqn.

# Variable Variables

 1   10–15 minutes

## Activity Overview

This is it—the moment you've been waiting for. Well, maybe not. But it's still exciting! You're going to store some variables in memory—the first real step in writing a program. Get ready to learn a little bit about what makes variables, well, variable, and how scoping affects them.

## Instructions

Setting variables in JavaScript is pretty easy. If you have experience in other languages, like Python, you'll notice that assigning variables is a little bit different. How, you say? Well, if you've skipped ahead in the book (how dare you!), you may have noticed all of these var keywords everywhere. What does it mean? It must have something to do with variables, right?

So, when you declare a variable like this in JavaScript:

```
myVar = 1;
```

It works fine, but there's an issue here. By not using the var keyword, we're creating myVar in the global scope. What does that mean? It means that myVar can be accessed from any other JavaScript code that's running in our ScriptCraft environment.

I know what you're thinking—what's the big deal? Well, you might like to live on the edge, but I don't. If we declare a variable in the global scope that has a really common name, like, say, "input," "output," "array," "file," etc., we run the risk of:

a) overwriting an existing variable that is likely an important part of a bigger system, or

b) having *our* variable overwritten by some other code that gets loaded after ours. Oops!

If we use var before we declare our variables, they'll be block scoped, which means that they're local to the block of code that contains them—this will be very important later. Basically, it means that the variables we declare (with var) are not going to be defined outside of the function/loop/IF statement that we declared them in.

Ok, so let's always use var! Here's how we should be declaring our variables:

```
// give it a try
var myVar = 1;
echo(self, myVar);
// 1
// variables in JS are mutable. Now try something like this
myVar = 2;
echo(self, myVar);
```

```
// 2
// we can declare variables and assign values to them later
var myUnassignedVar;
echo(self, myUnassignedVar);
// undefined
// we can assign variables to other variables
var myNewVar = myVar;
echo(self, myNewVar);
// 2
var myUnassignedVar = myNewVar;
echo(self, myUnassignedVar);
// 2
```

# Strings 'n' Things

 1    10–15 minutes

## Activity Overview

Strings are a really important data type in JavaScript. If you can remember all the way back to the beginning of the book (or just flip back), you'll know that strings are basically a bunch of characters "strung" together. You'll use them to represent a lot of things, like literal text, user input, configuration options, etc. Check out how they work!

## Instructions

Declaring a variable that holds a string in memory is pretty easy. It works like this:

```
var myString = 'this is a string';
echo(self, myString);
```

```
// this is a string
// Notice the single quotes? You can use double ones as well
myString = "this is a string with double quotes";
```

As you can see, you can put your strings in either single or double quotes. It doesn't really matter which you use—but you can't combine them:

```
var anotherString = 'this is a string";
// will give you an error!!
// you always need to wrap the string in quotes at the start and the end
var notActuallyAString = this is not a string
// this is not a string is not defined!
```

# Run the Numbers

 1    **10–15 minutes**

## Activity Overview

We've had a chance to look at strings, now we'll look at another major primitive in JavaScript: the number. JavaScript doesn't have any integers or floats. Instead, it's got an all-encompassing number type that is actually a double-precision floating point number. As cool as that title sounds, you don't need to know that—just remember that, by default, a number in JavaScript has a decimal. Go ahead and try your hand at numbers and let the computer do a little math for you.

## Instructions

Declaring a number looks like **this:**

```
var myNumber = 1;
echo(self, myNumber);
// 1
// right now it looks like an integer, but we can actually add a
decimal to it
myNumber + 0.005;
// 1.005
// you don't need to store numbers in variables to do arithmetic on
them
1 + 1;
// 2
5 * 5;
// 25
// we can add numbers stored in variables
var aNumber = 200;
var anotherNumber = 500;
aNumber + anotherNumber;
// 700
// by putting our statements in parentheses, we can respect the
order of operations
var someNumbers = (6 / 2) * 2;
// 6
// if we do it like this ...
var someNumbers = 6 / (2 * 2);
// 1.5
// we get a different result!
```

Now it's time to try your hand at messing with some numbers. We didn't go through all of the different arithmetic operators we touched on in chapter one—how about you try them? What kind of results did you get? Was it what you expected? Did you encounter any strange behavior?

# True or False

 1     10 minutes

## Activity Overview

Boolean values are pretty important. Even if we don't directly check to see if a value is true, there are several times we're doing it in a more implicit manner. We'll learn about that in a little bit. For now, we should just see what the deal is with Booleans—or true and false.

## Instructions

First, let's store some Boolean values in some variables and see what they behave like:

```
var myTrue = true;
var myFalse = false;
// that's it—that's all it takes! Easy. Let's see what they look like when
we log them
// also if you remember from the earlier section in the book, we can
check equality of variables with the "==" and "===" operators
echo(self, myTrue == true);
// true
echo(self, myFalse == false);
// true
echo(self, myTrue == false);
// false
// here is where it gets interesting
echo(self, 1 == true);
// true
echo(self, 0 == false);
// true
echo(self, 'true' == true)
// false
```

```
// WHAT!?
```

Check that out! Using the regular equality operator (==), 1 evaluates to true, and 0 evaluates to false. Any strings that we write evaluate to false when we check them like this. Even crazier is this:

```
echo (self, 1 === true);
// false
```

Because, if you remember, the strict evaluation operator (===) also evaluates against the type and its value. So, 1 is a number (duh), but it's not a Boolean, and therefore evaluates to false.

# Null and Void (or Undefined)

 1   10 minutes

## Activity Overview

Now we're going to look at more primitive types—null and undefined. Like I was saying earlier, the one you'll likely see the most is undefined, especially when you're just getting started. Null is less common but can prove to be a handy tool we can pull out of our back pocket when we need to!

## Instructions

Null and undefined values are a bit more straightforward than Booleans in JavaScript. Undefined will haunt our dreams at night. Case in point:

```
// We will see undefined when we forget to assign variables that we
reference—or if we spell them wrong
```

```
echo(self, aVarThatNeverWas);
// will get a big, nasty error
// so will this ...
var correctSpelling = 'something';
echo(self, correctSpellig);
// Ahh!
```

That big, crazy-looking error that comes up when we make those mistakes is called a stack trace, which provides us with useful information when a runtime error occurs. It shows a path that backtracks from where the error happened in the interpreter to the line of source code that caused it. Very handy indeed!

```
[12:52:02 WARN]:            at net.minecraft.server.v1_12_R1.MinecraftServer.t(MinecraftServer.java:679)
[12:52:02 WARN]:            at net.minecraft.server.v1_12_R1.MinecraftServer.run(MinecraftServer.java:577)
[12:52:02 WARN]:            at java.lang.Thread.run(Thread.java:748)
[12:52:02 WARN]: Caused by: <eval>:638:8 javax.script.ScriptException: ReferenceError: "aVarThatNeverWas" is not defined in <eval
[12:52:02 WARN]:            at jdk.nashorn.internal.runtime.ECMAException.create(ECMAException.java:113)
[12:52:02 WARN]:            at jdk.nashorn.internal.scripts.Script$Recompilation$3605$\^eval\._onEnable#__onCommand(<eval>:638)
[12:52:02 WARN]:            at jdk.nashorn.internal.runtime.ScriptFunctionData.invoke(ScriptFunctionData.java:628)
[12:52:02 WARN]:            at jdk.nashorn.internal.runtime.ScriptFunction.invoke(ScriptFunction.java:494)
[12:52:02 WARN]:            at jdk.nashorn.internal.runtime.ScriptRuntime.apply(ScriptRuntime.java:393)
[12:52:02 WARN]:            at jdk.nashorn.api.scripting.ScriptObjectMirror.callMember(ScriptObjectMirror.java:199)
[12:52:02 WARN]:            at jdk.nashorn.api.scripting.NashornScriptEngine.invokeImpl(NashornScriptEngine.java:386)
[12:52:02 WARN]:            ... 18 more
[12:52:02 WARN]: Caused by: javax.script.ScriptException: ReferenceError: "aVarThatNeverWas" is not defined in <eval> at line num
[12:52:02 WARN]:            at jdk.nashorn.api.scripting.NashornScriptEngine.throwAsScriptException(NashornScriptEngine.java:470)
[12:52:02 WARN]:            at jdk.nashorn.api.scripting.NashornScriptEngine.evalImpl(NashornScriptEngine.java:454)
[12:52:02 WARN]:            at jdk.nashorn.api.scripting.NashornScriptEngine.evalImpl(NashornScriptEngine.java:406)
[12:52:02 WARN]:            at jdk.nashorn.api.scripting.NashornScriptEngine.evalImpl(NashornScriptEngine.java:402)
[12:52:02 WARN]:            at jdk.nashorn.api.scripting.NashornScriptEngine.eval(NashornScriptEngine.java:155)
[12:52:02 WARN]:            at javax.script.AbstractScriptEngine.eval(AbstractScriptEngine.java:264)
[12:52:02 WARN]:            at jdk.nashorn.internal.scripts.Script$Recompilation$3605$\^eval\._onEnable#__onCommand(<eval>:613)
[12:52:02 WARN]:            ... 23 more
[12:52:02 WARN]: Caused by: <eval>:1 ReferenceError: "aVarThatNeverWas" is not defined
[12:52:02 WARN]:            at jdk.nashorn.internal.runtime.ECMAErrors.error(ECMAErrors.java:57)
[12:52:02 WARN]:            at jdk.nashorn.internal.runtime.ECMAErrors.referenceError(ECMAErrors.java:319)
[12:52:02 WARN]:            at jdk.nashorn.internal.runtime.ECMAErrors.referenceError(ECMAErrors.java:291)
[12:52:02 WARN]:            at jdk.nashorn.internal.objects.Global.__noSuchProperty__(Global.java:1441)
[12:52:02 WARN]:            at jdk.nashorn.internal.scripts.Script$3651$\^eval\.:program(<eval>:1)
[12:52:02 WARN]:            at jdk.nashorn.internal.runtime.ScriptFunctionData.invoke(ScriptFunctionData.java:637)
[12:52:02 WARN]:            at jdk.nashorn.internal.runtime.ScriptFunction.invoke(ScriptFunction.java:494)
[12:52:02 WARN]:            at jdk.nashorn.internal.runtime.ScriptRuntime.apply(ScriptRuntime.java:393)
[12:52:02 WARN]:            at jdk.nashorn.api.scripting.NashornScriptEngine.evalImpl(NashornScriptEngine.java:449)
[12:52:02 WARN]:            ... 28 more
```

Another instance where you'll see undefined is when you allocate space for a variable, but don't assign it any value.

```
var declaredButNotAssigned;
echo(self, declaredButNotAssigned)
// undefined—but without the crazy error
```

On to null now. JavaScript programmers have debated over its use for years. And what does that mean for you? Well, null can be used as a value that, well, explicitly represents nothing. When we first set a variable and we don't really know what its value is going to be (like if it's set later in the program), we can set its value to null so we can explicitly check for a null value if the property doesn't get set.

**var** myVal = **null**;
**// then later on we can explicitly check if myVal !== null and perform some logic**

A lot of libraries work this way. For instance, if there's a function that searches a database for a value and the value isn't there, it could return null. If we use this convention, we're explicitly stating that nothing was found—the variable should be set to null. Now, I should say that using this pattern is only good if you're consistent. If not, you'll have null and undefined(s) all over the place! That's going to get confusing pretty quick. The best thing to do is to pick a pattern that works for you and stick with it!

# Cracking the Case

 1    10 minutes

## Activity Overview

Now for a break from our regularly scheduled programming. By now, you must be wondering, "Why does this guy keep naming his variables likeThis?" That, my friends, is called camel case—like the humps on a camel. Because we can't (and shouldn't!) put spaces in our variable names, we have to have another way of breaking up words and making the names easier to read. We could just do something like this:

*thisismyvariable*

But that's kind of hard to read. By convention, JavaScript developers use camel case when naming functions and variables. When we get into classes, you'll see that we use Pascal case (named after the Pascal language), where both words, not just the first word, are capitalized. Other languages (like Python) prefer for you to use snake_case, where nothing is capitalized and words are separated by underscores. The whole point of doing this, besides attempting to make things easier to read (andThisJustLooksCool), is standardization. We need to try to make things as consistent as possible, which helps other coders and our future selves.

## Instructions

Based on the following types, create variables with names that not only tell us something about the variable, but are also typed in the given case. Check out this example:
Number (camel case)
**var** myInt = **1**;

Your turn!

- Boolean (snake case)
- String (Pascal case)
- Null (camel case)
- Undefined (snake case)
- String (camel case)
- Number (Pascal case)
- Boolean (camel case)
- Null (Pascal case)
- String (snake case)

# Playing with Primitives: Part 1—Determining Types

 1　⏱ 5 minutes

## Activity Overview

JavaScript has a lot of built-in functions that enable you to do cool things with primitive types. Before we get to those, it may not be a bad idea to take a look at the typeof operator, which actually tells us what type our variable is. In practice, you won't use this very often, but hey—it can't hurt to learn.

## Instructions

The typeof operator is a pretty handy way to figure out the type of the variable in question. For instance:

```
echo(self, typeof 1);
// number
```

Now here is your task, should you choose to accept it (and you should): Using the typeof statement, create one variable for every primitive type and store a value in it that represents that type. Once you've done that, use the typeof operator to check and see if you were correct. All right, I'm going to go get a coffee—let me know when you're done!

# Playing with Primitives: Part 2—Numbers

 1     5 minutes

## Activity Overview

Although we already messed around with some arithmetic operators a few activities back, here we'll look at a few built-in functions for dealing with numbers. This is only the tip of the iceberg, but they'll likely become key tools in your coding arsenal.

## Instructions

JavaScript has a math class (and not the boring kind) that is full of really useful fixed methods. Let's start with integers and move on from there. Wait—I know what you're going to say: "JavaScript numbers are all doubles, not integers! Fake news!" Well, we can actually use a couple of methods to give us a number that represents an integer, so when we display it, it looks like 1, and not 1.000000000000000. Be honest—the first number looks a lot better.

```
// let's say we want to round to an integer value from this expression
var myNum = 5 / 2;
echo(self, myNum);
>> 2.5
// using Math.floor we can round down
echo(self, Math.floor(myNum));
>> 2
// or using Math.ceil we can round up
echo(self, Math.ceil(myNum))
>> 3
// pretty neat—we could also use Math.round, which will round to
the nearest integer
```

```
echo(self, Math.round(myNum))
>> 3
// another example
echo(self, Math.round(2.3));
>> 2
// What if you want to get the largest value out of a bunch of
numbers?
echo(self, Math.max(1, 2, 3, 4));
>> 4
// Or the smallest?
echo(self, Math.min(1, 2, 3, 4));
// 1
// or getting the square root of a number
echo(self, Math.sqrt(9));
>> 3
// and finally, a random number between 0 and 1
echo(self, Math.random());
>> 0.43735427148084194
```

Sometimes, you also need to convert between numbers and strings. JavaScript numbers can be converted to strings via the toString method, and to convert them back, you can use parseInt and parseFloat.

```
// convert a number to a string
var myInt = 1;
var myIntToString = myInt.toString();
/* here is something really important—the "+" operator is what we
call "overloaded." Depending on the type, it can do different things
*/
// this will surprise you!
echo(self, myIntToString + myInt);
>> "11"
// whoa, weird! That's because the "+" is used to concatenate
strings—more on that in the next activity!
```

```
// to add them properly we need to use parseInt
echo(self, myInt + parseInt(myIntString, 10));
>> 2
// the "10" we pass to that function is the "base." No big deal, but
we're using base 10, which is how we normally count (base 10
means using numbers 0 to 9).
// we could use parseFloat too
echo(self, myInt + parseFloat(myIntString));
>> 2
```

# Playing with Primitives: Part 3—String Concatenation

 1    5 minutes

## Activity Overview

So we've covered the math class and numbers. Now it's time to give strings some attention! You're going to be coding a lot of strings as you start making your awesome *Minecraft* mod, but let's start with one of the most common—and weirdly named—operations: concatenation.

## Instructions

Remember that crazy moment in the last activity where we tried to add a number and a string representation of a number? Well, we were actually concatenating two strings, which is a fancy way of saying we joined them together:

```
var myString = "Hello";
var myOtherString = "World";
```

```
echo(self, myString + myOtherString);
>> HelloWorld
// notice how there's no spaces in there? We have to explicitly add a
space to one of the operands
myOtherString = " World";
echo(self, myString + myOtherString);
>> Hello World
// we can concatenate more than 2 strings together
echo(self, myString + myOtherString + "!");
    >> Hello World!
```

Another way to do some concatenation is to use a combination of the "+" and "=" operators. We can only do this with one string at a time:

```
myString += myOtherString;
// now, myString contains myOtherString
echo(self, myString);
>> 0
// this is the equivalent of doing this
myString = myString + myOtherString;
```

Now, how about a task? I have scrambled this message here:

'soon', 'pretty', 'will', *'Minecraft'*, 'we', 'writing', 'in', 'be', 'code', 'concatenate', 'first', 'need', 'but', 'we', 'to', 'strings', 'these'

Can you figure out how to concatenate these together for me using a combination of both of the operators we just looked at?

# Playing with Primitives: Part 4—Other String Methods

 1   5 minutes

## Activity Overview

JavaScript has a lot of built-in methods for processing strings. That's good news for you! We can convert strings from lower to upper case, search them, see how many letters they have, get the last letter, get the first letter, trim them, slice them, repeat them ... but this isn't a book about strings—and I hope you aren't trying to learn how to knit. Let's check out the major stuff.

## Instructions

Say we want to find out how many letters are in a string. We can use the length property:

```
echo(self, "hello".length);
>> 5
```

You can also extract a substring from within a string using the substring method. A substring is exactly what it sounds like: a string within a string.

```
//make our variable British
var elloGovnah = "hello".substring(1,5);
echo(self, elloGovnah);
>> ello
```

The substring method returns a substring of our "hello" string starting at index 1 (e) and ending at index 5 (o). (Don't forget that an index starts at 0, so you have to add 1 to the position you actually want!)

What if we want to make sure our word starts with a letter? It's easy!

```
echo(self, "hello".startsWith('h'));
>> true
// or ends with a letter
echo(self, "hello".endsWith('o'));
    // true
// how about seeing if it contains a letter anywhere
echo(self, "hello".indexOf('l'));
>> 2
```

Wait a second—what? A 2? Why not "true"? That's because we used the indexOf method, which—you guessed it—returns the index of the first occurrence of the query letter. Meaning? It's the position in the string where the letter occurs, not the letter itself.

And now for my personal favorite: the split method, which will lead us into our next activity on arrays. The split method splits a string at a given character index and returns an array of all the elements before and after every occurrence of that character. It does something like this—say we want to break up our "hello" at the "e":

```
// h <- | -> llo
var mySplit = "hello".split("e");
>> ["h", "llo"]
```

We end up with an array that looks like this: [h, llo]. It has two elements: the first being all of the characters before the "e" ("h"), and the second being all of the characters after it ("llo"). Note that the "e," the character to split on, is not included in the final array. That's important!

Alright, I need you to split some stuff for me. First, how about you split up "hello, world" so that it's broken into two words. Don't forget the space!

Next, I'd like you to split this string up into three individual sentences:

**I have to look through my inventory before I head to Blackrock Mountain I have three blocks of redstone, some glowstone dust, and a map maybe I need some snacks, too.**

# Collections: Arrays and Objects

We just got through a lot, didn't we?. Nice work! You may want to go and get yourself a Gatorade or something—programming can take a lot out of you, especially your fingers.

Now we'll look at some of the more advanced data structures JavaScript has to offer: arrays and objects. You will always have these tools in your back pocket once you learn them. Arrays and objects are essential for storing and moving data in your programs. Once you get the hang of them, you'll use them for everything.

We'll start with the basics first—constructing arrays and objects and looking at all of JavaScript's built-in methods for performing operations on them. Then we'll start to do some more practical stuff with ScriptCraft's awesome drone and items modules. We'll work on placing arrays of blocks, as well as creating a "wish list" data structure to store a bunch of items for different types of players.

# Getting Started with Arrays

 1    10–15 minutes

## Activity Overview

We're going get started with arrays for now. First we'll look at how to construct one, as well as how to add and remove elements. Buckle up!

## Instructions

There are multiple ways to construct arrays in JavaScript:

```
// with some prepopulated values
    var myArray = [1, 2, 3, 4];
    >> [1, 2, 3, 4]
// where 1, 2, 3, and 4 are the elements in the array
// you can also construct an empty array and add elements later
    var myArray = [];
    >> []
// to add items to the end of an array, you can "push" them onto the
end:
    myArray.push(1);
    >> [1]
// or to add them to the beginning, we can use "unshift"
    myArray.unshift(2);
    >> [2,1]
// cool, now to access the values, we can use their indices
    echo(self, myArray[0]);
    >> 2
// remember, arrays are zero indexed!
    echo(self, myArray[1]);
    >> 1
```

```
// now if we want to remove an element from the end
    var last = myArray.pop();
    echo(self, last);
    >> 1
// or to remove the first element
    var first = myArray.shift();
    echo(self, first);
    >> 2
// to get the length of an array (the number of elements) use its
length property
    echo(self, myArray.length);
    >> 0
// that's because we popped and shifted out our elements!
```

# Block Party

 1     10–15 minutes

## Activity Overview

There are a lot of times where you don't need to iterate over a whole array (I know, I know, I'll show you how to do that soon) and you need to access a value that's somewhere in the middle. Here, we're going to grab different blocks from an array of rainbow-colored blocks.

## Instructions

First thing's first: ScriptCraft has a ton of helpful modules we can work with. One that we will see a lot of is the blocks module, which stores all of *Minecraft's* block and item data values with nice, human-readable property names. Just so you know, this is where you can find the original data values: https://minecraft.gamepedia .com/Java_Edition_data_values.

Let's start off with the rainbow property, which is an array that holds the seven colors of the rainbow:

```
var rainbows = blocks.rainbow;
echo(self, rainbows);
>> 95:14
>> 95:1
...
```

// now we have an array of rainbow colors. Just to make sure, let's see how many there are:

```
echo(self, rainbows.length);
>> 7
```

// so now, if we want to access one of the values that's not at the beginning or end, we can access it by its index

```
echo(self, rainbows[3])
>> 95:5
```

// which is the 4th element in the array. Why? Because they're zero indexed. I'm going to keep reminding you! I don't quit.

Great, so we can access some blocks. Big deal! Well, I know you're not impressed yet, but you will be. Why don't we actually add some of those blocks to our world?

To add blocks, we'll be using ScriptCraft's drone module, which is kind of like a robot we can program to move around the world and build structures. For now, we're just going to create a new drone instance and lay down some of our rainbow blocks.

```
// to create a new drone object instance, you use the
drone constructor
var drone = new Drone(self);
```

The drone constructor takes either a location (more on that later) or your self variable as a parameter. It returns a new drone at either your current location (self.location) or the location you pass in. There's plenty of time for us to get into this drone stuff, but we'll keep it pretty simple for now. Let's this just drop a block at our crosshairs.

drone.box(rainbows[**3**]);

This places a 1x1x1 green block right at our crosshairs—great! Let's do another:

drone.box(rainbows[**1**]);

Try to drop blocks of all the other colors. You can place them on top of each other, or wherever you want. Next, we'll learn how to drop a bunch in succession.

# Keys, Values, and Objects

 1 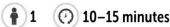 10–15 minutes

## Activity Overview

Don't worry, we haven't seen the last of our good friend Mr. Array, I just want us to get acquainted with another good friend, Ms. Object, which is absolutely essential to the core of understanding JavaScript. I know, I'm blowing things out of proportion—or am I?

## Instructions

At their simplest, JavaScript objects are just key-value pairs. Unlike the array, which has numerical indices, objects have values that are indexed by keys. These keys are usually strings, but they can be numbers too.

```
// constructing an empty object
var myObject = {};
// we can set keys and values like this
```

```
myObject['key'] = "value";
// we could also set them using the dot operator
myObject.key = "value";
// we can also access them the same way
echo(self, myObject.key);
>> "value"
echo(self, myObject['key']);
>> "value"
// as you can see here, the properties are mutable—we can keep
changing them
myObject.key = "cat"
echo(self, myObject.key);
>> "cat"
// it's also important to note that keys need to be unique, or else
you run the risk of uninentionally replacing their values
```

We can also use what are called object literals, which are handy if we already have known values we want to set:

```
var literal = { key: "value" };
// note how "key" didn't have to be in quotes there
// to add multiple properties, separate them by a comma
literal = { key: "value", otherKey: "other value" };
// we can add more properties by index or by the dot operator,
although the latter is more common
literal.anotherKey = "another value"
```

Remember when I said, "I don't want anybody to know my inventory?" I lied. Can you make me an object with the following properties?

```
Glowstone dust: 5,
Redstone blocks: 3,
Map: 1
```

# Wish List

  1    ⏱ 10–15 minutes

## Activity Overview

You probably think you're pretty good at objects by now, and you are. But let's keep improving those object skills by exploring ScriptCraft's items module, which, like the blocks module, nicely maps item data values to human-readable properties. We're going to compile a wish-list object of all of the items we wish we could put in our inventory.

## Instructions

The items module is one big object where each "key" or property is an item type. Unlike with the blocks module, however, the properties aren't really properties at all. They're actually methods— static methods, to be precise. When we start to get into writing our own classes and prototypes, methods should make more sense. For now, we're not going to worry about their inner workings. We just want to get some stuff!

We're going to do something new here. Because the items module isn't loaded by default, we have to explicitly load it ourselves. Thankfully, ScriptCraft uses a require module that works like the one in NodeJS. To load a module, we type this:

```
var items = require('items');
// let's start by creating our wish-list object:
var wishlist = {};
```

Each method in the items module returns either a single material corresponding to an item or an ItemStack, which is a Java class that contains multiple items.

```
// to get one item
echo(self, items.book());
>> BOOK
//returns a material of type BOOK
//if we pass a number as a parameter, we get n books
echo(self, items.book(2));
>> ItemStack{ BOOK x 2 }
```

Because objects can store any value as a property, we can actually store the return values of the item methods in our wish list. For instance, if I want 5 books:

```
wishlist.books = items.book(5);
echo(self, wishlist.books);
>> ItemStack{ BOOK x 5 }
```

All of the items we're capable of accessing can be found here: https://hub.spigotmc.org/javadocs/spigot/org/bukkit/Material.html
Keep in mind that everything in the items module is camel cased, so if you want to add a SLIME_BALL to your wish list you would use the items.slimeBall method. Ok, now go get that wish list together!

That's the first time you've seen a variable name in ALL_CAPS with the separator as an underscore. Well, all of those item materials are what we call constants. A constant is a special variable whose value doesn't change (also known as immutable), and whose name can only be declared once. The convention of naming constants all in capitals is a common one shared by many languages. Nashorn, unfortunately, doesn't have support for constants at the time I'm writing this, but ES6 JavaScript does. As you'll see later, we can at least state our intentions that a variable is a constant if we name it LIKE_THIS. If we do, other developers who see our code should respect the convention and leave it alone.

There you have it, folks—arrays and objects! This definitely won't be the last we'll see of them. We're actually just getting started! Once we move on to control flow and iteration, you'll be able to witness the real power of these data structures firsthand. As you can already see, programming concepts all build off one another. The more you learn, the larger your toolset will be. It's just like your inventory in *Minecraft*—you can combine data structures, functions, and patterns to make really cool and useful stuff!

# Control Flow, Plus an IDE!

Now it's time to control the flow of our code. We're going to look at the IF statement, a very important piece of code that allows us to put logic into our programs. After that, we're going to have to take a slight detour to set up an IDE (integrated development environment—basically just a fancy name for a text editor) so we can write code that stretches beyond one line. This is an unfortunate limitation of *Minecraft*'s command prompt—but as you'll see, it's way easier for us to write all our code in a file and import it into ScriptCraft and run it that way.

We'll also look at the switch statement, which is an alternative way of writing branching code. We'll also set up a custom ScriptCraft plugin that we can use to store all our code in. This is shaping up great! We're really starting to make some progress here—every activity is taking you one step closer to your *Minecraft* mod.

# The Mighty IF Statement

 1    10–15 minutes

## Activity Overview

Now that you have data types down, it's time to try your hand at some logic. As you already know, we use IF statements to control the flow of our programs, allowing them to branch out and execute different tasks based on some conditions.

We'll play around with the IF statement and come up with some custom wish lists based how we plan on playing *Minecraft*.

## Instructions

Based off your wish list from the last activity, I'd like you to come up with three small wish lists for three types of generic players: a player who wants to go on quests, a player who wants to build things, and a player who just wants to explore. Store them in variables called *questList*, *buildList*, and *exploreList*.

Now what you're going to do is pretend that a new user has entered some info to specify the type of player that he or she is. That info will be stored in a *playerType* variable.

```
// for instance
var playerType = 'quest';
// other options could be 'build' and 'explore'
// let's start by declaring an empty wish list
var wishlist = null;
```

Remember, we explicitly declare the wish list as null so we can check for it later. This also states our intention that the wish list is going to be empty until we decide what type of list the player should have. This is based on the way he or she wants to play the game!

Now, for a quick (but necessary) detour. So far, we've been writing code that can all fit on one line in the command prompt. Unfortunately, the prompt is not set up to handle any code that goes across multiple lines. This is actually fine in JavaScript because the interpreter doesn't care about new lines or white space unlike some other languages. For this activity, you're going to write your IF statements on a single line, but starting with the next activity, you're actually going to start writing your stuff in an IDE so that it'll be clearer for you to read and understand—plus you can save your work!

Now that I've gotten that out of the way, let's write our first IF statement.

```
if (playerType === 'quest') { wishlist = questList; }
echo(self, wishlist === null);
>> false
// this means our list was properly set to an object because it's not null anymore!
```

There's quite a bit to unpack in that little block of code. First is the IF statement, which looks like this:

```
if (condition) { code that gets executed }
```

So IF that condition is met, the computer will execute whatever is in the curly brackets. If the condition isn't met, the computer moves along to the rest of the program. Let's see what happens if we change our playerType and use that same if statement as before:

```
playerType = 'lazy';
if (playerType === 'quest') { wishlist = questList; }
echo(self, wishlist === null);
>> true
```

See, the program just skipped on ahead and ignored that block in the IF statement. Got it? Now try to change your player types and write IF statements for the other two lists.

# Setting Up an IDE

 1    10–15 minutes    Atom or your favorite IDE/text editor

## Activity Overview

We're going to take the time to download and install an IDE to help us write our code and organize our projects. We will be installing GitHub's Atom IDE, which is a good open-source program (and, better yet, it's free). I'll also provide you with a list of alternatives in case you don't like Atom.

## Instructions

### To install Atom

1. Download Atom from https://atom.io
   a. On a Mac, open up the DMG file and move Atom to your Applications folder.
   b. On Windows, open and run the installer

### To open a project folder

1. Click on File → Add Project Folder.
2. Navigate to your spigotmc directory.
3. Open the ScriptCraft directory.
4. Click on the plugins folder and select Open.

### To create a new file

1. Now, on the left-hand side, you should see a section called Folders. Underneath should be the plugins folder. There are a number of subfolders in there, as well as JavaScript files with the extension .js. Right-click the plugins folder icon and select New -> File

2. You should be prompted to give the file a name. Let's make it something unique so we can tell it apart from the other files. How about {your name}-exercises.js? So, my file would be josh-exercises.js. Great! Now we can start adding our code to the file and running it right in *Minecraft*!

If you don't really like Atom as an IDE, here is a list of others with links. Note—we won't be doing anything Atom specific to make our *Minecraft* mod, so you can use whichever text editor you like:

- VSCode: https://code.visualstudio.com
- Sublime Text: https://www.sublimetext.com
- WebStorm: https://www.jetbrains.com/webstorm
- TextWrangler (Mac): https://www.barebones.com/products/textwrangler
- Notepad++ (Windows): https://notepad-plus-plus.org

# Creating a ScriptCraft Plugin

 1    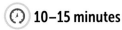 10–15 minutes     Atom or your favorite IDE/text editor

## Activity Overview

Because the *Minecraft* console only lets us write our code on a single line, we're going to write a quick function that will allow us to run more complex, multi-line code. We'll briefly touch on writing functions here, but you'll have to wait until a bit later to really dive in!

Everything in the scriptcraft/plugins folder gets loaded into *Minecraft* every time ScriptCraft is refreshed. This means that all of the functions we write in our {your name}-exercises.js will be in the global namespace. Meaning? Remember when we talked about using var to block scope our variables so we don't "pollute" the global namespace? Well this is the opposite of that—all of our function names and variables will be global. What we can do instead is write an object that contains local functions—basically all of our exercises from here on in. That way, we won't run into any conflicts. It sounds confusing, but trust me, it's not that bad!

# Instructions

Let's open up that {your-name}-exercises.js file. We're going to create an object literal, but it's going to look a little different from what we're used to:

```
exports.exercises = {};
```

What we're doing here is adding our exercises to the exports global object, which allows for everything in our exercises object to be loaded into ScriptCraft automatically. Now, I'm actually going to change that code slightly—we're going to put all of our functions in the object literal like this:

```
exports.exercises = {
    helloWorld: function() {
            // the code for our helloWorld function goes here
    }
}
```

Remember, functions are just modular blocks of code that we can call by name. For the next few exercises, none of our functions are going to take any arguments or parameters, and they're not going to return anything—they'll just execute our code. Let's modify our helloWorld function to echo something to the screen:

```
exports.exercises = {
    helloWorld: function() {
            echo(self, "I can't believe this actually worked!");
    }
}
```

Now, if we go back into *Minecraft* and open the console, we just have to type:

/js refresh();

This will reload all of the ScriptCraft plugins. Now we should be able to call our function from the console:

/js exercises.helloWorld()
>> "I can't believe this actually worked!"

That's what I'm talking about! Now we can work on more complicated programs and save our work!

When we want to add more exercises, we just separate them by a comma:

```
exports.exercises = {
    helloWorld: function() {
        echo(self, "I can't believe this actually worked!");
    },
    anotherExercise: function() {
        echo(self, "I'm less impressed now since I know it
    works");
    }
}
```

# Branching Out

## Activity Overview

Believe it or not, we did all that just to set up this activity. That was a lot—but hey, now we're set! We're going to push this wish list example a few steps further by adding some branching logic using IF, ELSE-IF, and else statements.

## Instructions

Let's create a new function in our exercises object literal and call it ifStatement.

```
exports.exercises = {
    helloWorld: function() {
        echo(self, "I can't believe this actually worked!");
    },
    ifStatement: function() {
        // code goes here
    }
}
```

Now, we're going to place our three wish lists in that ifStatement function. Remember, we need three object literals with specifically curated items for each: *build, quest, and explore.* You should also add a fourth, called *generic*. This is going to be our default wish list if our hypothetical user doesn't want to be stuck with one of the others. You can just put a few random items in there. You should also add one more property to each of them. We're going to assign them a type property so we can check and see what type of wish list we actually have. Now you should have something like this:

```
var build = {
    // build items go here
    type: "build",
}

var quest = {
    // quest items go here
    type: "quest",
}

var explore = {
    // explore items go here
    type: "explore",
}

var generic = {
    // generic items go here
    type: "generic",
}
```

Excellent! Remember, because we're using var, all of these objects are local to our ifStatement function and won't be loaded into ScriptCraft's global namespace by default. So now let's just set a dummy variable for our playerType and initialize a null wish list:

```
var playerType = "build";
var wishlist = null;
```

Now we can write our conditional statements. Let's start with one we've already done:

```
// ah it feels good to be able to program on multiple lines
if (playerType === "build") {
    wishlist = build;
}
```

Now, we could just add multiple IF statements like that to our code and we could almost achieve our desired effect:

**\* Don't forget to hit refresh before you run exercises.ifStatement() \***
```
if (playerType === "build") {
        wishlist = build;
}
if (playerType === "quest") {
        wishlist = quest;
}
if (playerType === "explore") {
        wishlist = explore;
}
```

But where do we set our generic wish list? We want it to be the default wish list if there's no user input at all. Hmm. Well, you can tack on an else branch to an IF statement. That else branch will be executed if the condition isn't met, remember?

```
var playerType = "build";
var wishlist = null;
if (playerType === "build") {
        wishlist = build;
}
if (playerType === "quest") {
        wishlist = quest;
}
if (playerType === "explore") {
        wishlist = explore;
} else {
        wishlist = generic;
}
// let's see how we did
echo(self, wishlist.type);
>> "generic"
```

What? NO! What happened? Well, the way we set up that IF statement doesn't quite replicate our goal. This is how the program is currently flowing:

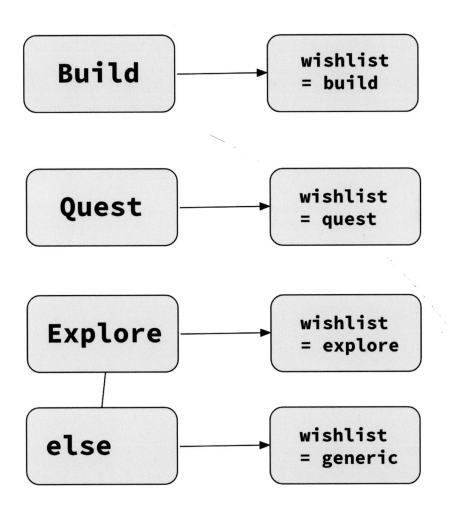

if player type is build --> set wish list to build
if player type is quest --> set wish list to quest
if player type is explore --> set wish list to explore
if player type is not explore --> set wish list to generic

Oops. Can you spot the problem? Because each IF statement is being executed independent of the other, the else branch is only attached to the if (*playerType* === *"explore"*) condition. Even if our wish list is set to build, it eventually gets set to generic because the playerType isn't "explore." Get it? Try changing playerType to "explore" and you'll see what I mean—you should have a wish list of type "explore" now.

What we should have done was use ELSE-IF statements, which will actually link the statements together, and the else branch will only execute if playerType is not build, quest, or explore:

```
var playerType = "build";
var wishlist = null;
if (playerType === "build") {
        wishlist = build;
} else if (playerType === "quest") {
        wishlist = quest;
} else if (playerType === "explore") {
        wishlist = explore;
} else {
        wishlist = generic;
}
// let's try it again
echo(self, wishlist.type);
        >> "build"
```

Yes! We did it!

# The Old Switcheroo

 1   20–25 minutes   Atom or your favorite IDE/text editor

## Activity Overview

We're going to take the previous IF … ELSE-IF … else workflow and convert it to a switch statement. Sounds exciting, right? What, don't you think so? Well it's pretty cool because you'll soon discover that there are multiple ways to solve the same problem—and one solution is often not any "better" than the other.

## Instructions

Let's start by adding a function called switchCase to our exercises.

```
exports.exercises = {
    helloWorld: function() {
        // code goes here
    },
    ifStatement: function() {
        // code goes here
    },
    switchCase: function() {
        // code goes here
    }
}
```

Don't forget that all of these functions need to be separated by a comma! Although there are better ways to do this, for now let's just copy and paste our wish lists from the ifStatement function into this one. Now we should have something like this:

```javascript
var build = {
    // build items go here
    type: "build",
}
var quest = {
    // quest items go here
    type: "quest",
}
var explore = {
    // explore items go here
    type: "explore",
}
var generic = {
    // generic items go here
    type: "generic",
}
```

Now, we'll set our wish list variable to null and add a playerType variable set to "build." Let's also lay the groundwork of our switch.

```javascript
var playerType = "build";
var wishlist = null;
switch (playerType) {
    // cases go here
}
```

First thing's first—the switch statement takes an expression as a parameter. It will always be the variable you're trying to check against, which in our case is playerType. We then write our cases within the curly brackets—our cases are like the (playerType === "build") conditions of the IF statements:

```javascript
switch (playerType) {
    case "build":
```

```
        wishlist = build;
        break;
    case "quest":
        wishlist = quest;
        break;
    case "explore":
        wishlist = explore;
        break;
    default:
        wishlist = generic;
        break;
    }
echo(self, wishlist.type);
>> "build"
```

Most of that stuff is pretty self-explanatory—with the exception of those break statements. So, for the matching case, all of the code after the ":" is executed. Unlike an IF statement, we have to use that break statement to explicitly "break out" of that switch and get back to executing the rest of our code. Also, you'll notice that default case—it serves the exact same purpose as our "else" in the last activity. Pretty easy, right?

You've heard of air traffic controllers, right? Well, after that section, you're like a code traffic controller! You now know how to control the flow of your programs. IF and switch statements may still feel a little awkward, but as you start to practice with them, they'll become second nature. Practice will also give you the skills to understand which one works best in a given scenario. Like I was saying before, there isn't necessarily a right way and a wrong way of solving problems with programming, especially when you're first starting out. There may be instances where there's a better way, and if you're struggling, you're in good company! Even professional programmers are constantly looking to find ways to improve the performance and readability of their code.

# Iteration

I hope you're hungry because now we're starting to get into the meat of programming! Along with branching logic (IF statements), iteration is one of the major pillars of programming. It really is what makes programming so powerful. Think about it: let's say you need to rename five hundred files in a directory and move them somewhere else. That would not only a) take a long time, but b) be incredibly tedious and prone to human error. Computers never get tired, and iteration is what makes them work!

We'll start with the FOR loop, which is arguably the most commonly used form of iteration. We'll also look at the while loop, iterating over objects with for ... in, and some functional programming with the Array.forEach method. To get all that done, we'll also start looking at functions because we need to use them with Array.forEach. We'll look at some more practical examples with ScriptCraft. Ever wanted to stock your inventory with stuff? We'll do that. Ever wanted to blow up every monster on your map? We'll do that, too. All with the power of iteration!

# The Mighty FOR Loop

 1   15–20 minutes   Atom or your favorite IDE/text editor

## Activity Overview

Enough with all of this "doing things one at a time" stuff. That's so one page ago. Maybe two. Either way, once we learn how to write loops, our lives will change forever. Okay, maybe I'm overstating it ... But I'm definitely not. The FOR loop is one of the many ways we can handle iteration in JavaScript. It may be the most complicated, but it's the fastest, performance wise.

## Instructions

You know the drill—add another function to that exercises object called forLoop. We're going to go back to our trusty blocks.rainbow array and iterate over it. A FOR loop looks like this:

```
for (var i = 0; i < blocks.rainbow.length; i++) {
        // code to run at every iteration goes here
}
```

Whoa, that looks kind of complicated, doesn't it? Let's break down what's going on inside those parentheses.

- var i = 0;—We could give this variable another name, but you'll likely see "i" a lot. Why? Well, the variable that we're actually setting is our *index* in the FOR loop, and index starts with "i". You could also call it "index," but shorter variable names are easier in something like a FOR loop since we're referring to our index a lot.

- So now we know, "i" is our index and we're setting it at 0—the beginning of the array.
- i < blocks.rainbow.length;—This is the condition that we check at every iteration, and what tells the interpreter that it's time to stop iterating and break out of the loop. Basically all we're doing is saying: keep iterating as long as our index is smaller than the size of the array.
- i++—This is where we increment our index by 1 after every iteration. This is really important—if we don't set it, we end up with an infinite loop, which will lock up our program and make it run forever. That sounds really cool—but it isn't useful for us right now.

Inside the curly brackets, we have access to our "i" variable, which we can then use to access elements from our blocks .rainbow array based on the current value of our index. For instance, in our first iteration, the value of our index is 0. This means that we can grab the first element in the blocks.rainbow array by its index:

```
for (var i = 0; i < blocks.rainbow.length; i++) {
    var currentBlock = blocks.rainbow[i];
    // do something with currentElement
}
```

There you have it—that's one way you can iterate over an array and access all of its elements. Let's visualize it with a drone.

We can initialize the drone outside of the FOR loop, as we don't need to construct one for every iteration:

```
var d = new Drone(self);
// drone is at our current location
for (var i = 0; i < blocks.rainbow.length; i++) {
    var currentBlock = blocks.rainbow[i];
```

```
    // move forward one block every iteration and drop one block
of the current color
    d.fwd().box(currentBlock); //an example of method chaining
}
```

If all goes according to plan, you should see a line of seven different-colored blocks appear before you. If that's not magical, I don't know what is.

# The Mighty While Loop

 1     10–15 minutes     Atom or your favorite IDE/text editor

## Activity Overview

Not to be outdone, the while loop is just as amazing as the FOR loop. Hope you liked the last activity because here it is again—this time using a while loop. You'll see for yourself that the two are a little different. Deciding on which one to use—and when—is something that comes with practice. Like everything else, however, one way isn't better than the other, it just might be better suited for the situation at hand.

## Instructions

Create a new function in exercises and call it whileLoop. Go ahead and set up a drone, as well as an index variable.

```
var d = new Drone(self);
var i = 0; // wait, we don't declare this in the while loop?
```

No, we don't. The while loop runs while a condition is met. We just pass the while loop the condition. If you remember back to the last section, we have to handle the incrementing of our index (i) ourselves.

```
var d = new Drone(self);
var i = 0;
while(i < blocks.rainbow.length) {
    // the same code as before
    var currentBlock = blocks.rainbow[i];
    // move forward one block every iteration and drop one block
    of the current color
    d.fwd().box(currentBlock); // an example of method chaining
```

```
// with one important addition:
i++; // don't forget this! Otherwise I will loop
forever! Muahahaha!
}
```

# Populating an Inventory (AKA Cheating)

 1   25–30 minutes

## Activity Overview

Remember those wish lists we compiled a while back? Well, they're back again! We're going to clean up our code a little bit so we can adhere to the DRY principle (don't repeat yourself) so we don't have to keep copying and pasting them into our functions. Once we do that, we're going to learn how to iterate over object properties and actually populate our inventory with items from the wish lists. Yes, you can actually do that!

## Instructions

Let's take a look at our exercises object. Instead of copying and pasting our wish lists into multiple functions, is there any way we can just write them once and access them from all of our functions? If you thought "why don't we store them as a property in our exercises object," you get a gold star! We can have deeply nested objects, meaning that one object can contain another object, which can contain another object ...

Let's add an object literal to the top of our exercises object called wishLists, and add all of our wish lists to that:

```
exports.exercises = {
 wishLists: {
    build: { /* all of your build items */ },
    quest: { /* all of your quest items */ },
    explore: { /* all of your explore items */ },
    generic: { /* all of your generic items */ }
 },
 // all other exercises go here
}
```

Now, any time we want to access those in our exercises, we call exercises.wishLists; for a specific wish list, we call exercises. wishLists.build, and so on and so forth.

Let's make another exercise function below the others and call it populateInventory. The first thing we need to do is load the inventory module. We'll need it again in our exercises, so let's "require" it at the top of our file. While we're at it, we need to load the items module, too, because our wish lists rely on it.

```
var inventory = require('inventory');
var items = require('items');
// everything else is below this
```

So, where does one begin? Let's access our inventory and store a reference to it in a variable:

```
var myInventory = inventory(self);
```

The inventory module consists of one function that takes a player or NPC (nonplayer character) as an argument. It returns an object that represents the inventory for that player or NPC and contains three methods: add, remove, and contains. Let's also store a reference to our build wish list so we don't need to keep typing out exercises.wishLists.build:

```
// for now we'll populate our inventory with the build wish list items
var buildWishList = exercises.wishLists.build;
// that will save us some typing
```

Now we're ready to iterate over the wish list! To do it, we'll use a for ... in loop. This is a fairly recent addition to Nashorn and it's pretty handy. It looks like this:

```
for (var key in buildWishList) {
        // do something with key here
}
```

Wow, that's a lot clearer than a regular for loop. A for ... in loop iterates over the properties of an object. It doesn't give us the value of the object, but the name of the property (its key—that explains the variable name), which we can then use to access the corresponding value from buildWishList. For example:

```
for (var key in buildWishList) {
        echo(self, "Key: " + key);
        echo(self, "Value: " + buildWishList[key]);
}
```

You should get all of the keys and values for your build wish list. Pretty cool! Now for the final piece of the puzzle, let's call myInventory's add method and add every item in our wish list:

```
for (var key in buildWishList) {
        myInventory.add(buildWishList[key]);
}
```

Congratulations, you are now flush with items—no need to thank me!

# forEach: Part 1—The Callback

 1     20–25 minutes    ✖ Atom or your favorite IDE/text editor

## Activity Overview

There's yet another way to iterate over an array in JavaScript, and it may be a little more difficult to understand than the last two. I think you'll get it, but you better buckle up! In JavaScript, an array actually has a method called forEach, which iterates over every element in the array and calls a supplied function on each individual element. This function is what's known as a callback, which is a function that is passed as an argument to another function and is called from the function it was passed to. It sounds confusing, but once you see it in action, it'll make a lot more sense.

Since we've been doing all of this happy-go-lucky rainbow stuff, let's use a forEach method to do something a little ... darker. We're going to go ahead and blow up every entity in our world! Muahahahaha! First, we need to write the callback, which is going to create an explosion at every entity's location.

## Instructions

In part 2 of this activity, we'll write the forEach method that will supply our function with the entity information we need. But first, let's create a new function in our exercises object called forEach.

All right, now this is the first time we'll be defining a function that takes an argument. Let's call it blowUpEntity.

```
// defining a named function with 1 argument
function blowUpEntity(entity) {
    // blow stuff up
}
```

This example would be called a unary function because we're passing one (get it? Like "uno"?) argument to it. If you want to pass more than one entity into a function, you just have to put it inside the parentheses. For example:

```javascript
// passing in the power of the explosion
function blowUpEntity(entity, power) {
      // blow stuff up
}
```

The forEach method actually passes three arguments to its provided callback: the element, the index of the element, and the array that the forEach method is actually being called on. For now, we're only concerned with the entity. Each entity has a location property, which we're going to use as the location for our explosion. The createExplosion method actually belongs to the World class, which we can get from our self variable.

```javascript
var world = self.world;
function blowUpEntity(entity) {
    // blow stuff up
    // location, power, setFire
    world.createExplosion(entity.location, 1.0, true);
```

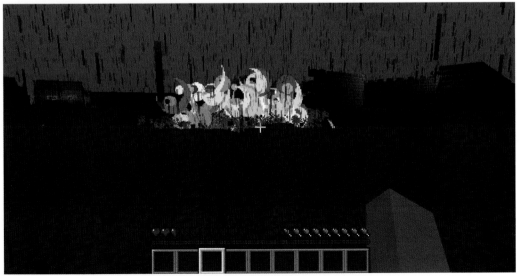

There, that's all we need to type to cause all kinds of destruction and property damage ... In *Minecraft* only, of course.

The World class has a boatload of methods and properties that are useful to us. Check out the SpigotMC API if you don't believe me: https://hub.spigotmc.org/javadocs/spigot/org/bukkit/World .html. Give some of the methods a try and see what happens!

# forEach: Part 2—The Method

 1     **15–20 minutes**    ✖ **Atom or your favorite IDE/text editor**

## Activity Overview

In the previous activity, we wrote a function to blow up an entity at its location. Now, we're going to use the forEach method to blow up ALL of the entities in our world. We're going to use another method from the World class to get all of the entities.

## Instructions

So far, we should have this:

```
var world = self.world;
function blowUpEntity(entity) {
    // blow stuff up
    // location, power, setFire
    world.createExplosion(entity.location, 1.0, true);
}
```

Since we declared that blowUpEntity function in the scope of our forEach exercise function, it's only available locally. Which is good because with great power comes great responsibility!

To get all of the entities in our world, we just call the getEntities method.

```
var entities = world.getEntities();
```

WAIT! Our character is an entity, too. Thankfully, there's a different method: getEntitiesByClass. We're going to have put in a little bit of elbow grease here to avoid exploding ourselves (but if you're feeling reckless, you can try the above method).

One of the really great things about ScriptCraft and Nashorn is that we can import Java classes and functions into our JavaScript code. Because the getEntitiesByClass method requires a Java class type as a parameter, we'll have to import the class into our program. Let's say we only want to blow up all of the monsters (pigs and horses never hurt anybody).

To load a Java class in JavaScript, we do this:

```
var Monster = Java.type('org.bukkit.entity.Monster');
```

That successfully loads in the Monster type from the Entity package. Now, we just have to get an array with all of the monsters:

```
// the Monster.class property is kind of like typeof in JavaScript
var entities = getEntitiesByClass(Monster.class);
entities.forEach(blowUpEntity);
```

That's pretty much it—when we call our forEach exercise function, you'll probably start to see, and hear, a lot of explosions. Make sure you're not standing too close to any monsters!

Just for reference, here is the full code:

```
forEach: function() {
    var world = self.world;
    var Monster = Java.type('org.bukkit.entity.Monster');
    function blowUpEntity(entity) {
    world.createExplosion(entity.location, 1.0, true);
    }
    var zombies = world.getEntitiesByClass(Monster.class);
    zombies.forEach(blowUpEntity);
}
```

Wow! Iteration is pretty cool, isn't it? You're probably thinking about all the crazy stuff you'll be able to do now. And if not, let your creativity run wild! You just unlocked a door to endless iteration possibilities.

Just like with IF and switch statements, there isn't necessarily a right or wrong way to do iteration. The important thing is to make everything clear and consistent. Before we move on to the next subsection, maybe you can take some time to play around with iteration a bit more. It's one of the tougher concepts to grasp, but all of this stuff is like riding a bike. With more and more practice, you'll be a pro in no time!

# Functions and Event-Driven Programming

JavaScript has support for several programming paradigms, including object-oriented programming, functional programming, and event-driven programming. In this section, we'll delve deeper into functions, which help us to clean up our code and make it more modular. We'll also take a look at event-driven programming, which is a big part of software development—including games. Why, you ask? You never know what kind of kind of choices a player is going to make, and games these days are pretty nonlinear. With events, we can wait and listen for specific things to happen and then handle them accordingly. The way we handle those specific things (or events, like in the name) is by using functions. See how it's all coming together?

# Return to Sender

 1    15–20 minutes    Atom or your favorite IDE/text editor

## Activity Overview

You must be pretty good at writing functions by now. One thing we haven't touched on yet, however, is writing a function that returns something. Returning a value from a function is like sticking some money in a vending machine and getting some chips back. Except, you'll probably still be hungry after your function runs.

So far, we've utilized functions that have return values and stored those in variables. Functions can return anything—strings, arrays, objects—even other functions! We're going to extend this vending machine metaphor even further and create a function that returns a user-defined number of a specified item.

## Instructions

The first step is to create our function—we'll call it functionReturn. It's going to look a little different this time because it's going to take two parameters, or arguments:

```
functionReturn: function(itemType, nItems) {
    // code to return n items
}
```

This one should be pretty easy! All the user has to do is pass in the name of the item type in a camel-cased string—I'm in the mood for a bakedPotato—and the amount of baked potatoes he or she wants:

```
functionReturn: function(itemType, nItems) {
    return items[itemType](nItems);
}
```

It may look a little wild, but what we're doing is really straightforward. We're accessing the itemType value from the items object by using the supplied property, or key. We're then calling the value, which is a method, with the number of items as a parameter. Let's see what happens when we run the code in *Minecraft*:

```
var potatoes = exercises.functionReturn('bakedPotato', 20);
echo(self, potatoes);
>> ItemStack{BAKED_POTATO x 10}
```

Pretty neat, but kind of boring. Why don't we go ahead and have our function return another function that will actually drop nPotatoes right at our location whenever we call it.

```
functionReturn: function(itemType, nItems) {
    // our world
    var world = self.world;
    var itemStack = items[itemType](nItems);
    return function() {
        /* we can use dropItem, which takes a location and an
        itemStack as arguments */
        world.dropItem(self.location, itemStack);
    }
}
```

Now, to actually use that function, we can store the return value in variable with a name that makes more sense:

```
var gimmePotatoes = exercises.functionReturn('bakedPotato', 20);
```

Now, as we're walking around, we can just call 'gimmePotatoes' whenever we want.

gimmePotatoes(); // instantly gives me twenty baked potatoes! Pass the butter!

Okay, now I'm getting sick of potatoes—what if we don't always want twenty? Can we switch it up? Oh, you bet we can:

```
functionReturn: function(itemType) {
    var world = self.world;
    // now nItems gets passed to the returned function instead
    return function(nItems) {
        var itemStack = items[itemType](nItems);
        world.dropItem(self.location, itemStack);
    }
}
//in Minecraft
var gimmePotatoes = exercises.functionReturn('bakedPotato');
gimmePotatoes(1);
//ah, only one, much better
```

# Mr. Anonymous

 1    15–20 minutes    Atom or your favorite IDE/text editor

## Activity Overview

We're going to take care of two concepts in this activity—we'll get started with event-driven programming in order to listen to events that get dispatched (sent) from SpigotMC. We'll also use anonymous functions to react to these events.

Event-driven programming is another paradigm central to JavaScript, where events are emitted, or dispatched, as a result of some type of input or user action. The events are intercepted by listeners, which in turn fire a callback function (CB) that often takes information about the event as a parameter. That sounds pretty complicated. So forget that—think about it in a simpler way. Imagine a message passing: a message is sent to all recipients waiting for the message, and each one does something after he or she has received the message.

It's pretty common to use anonymous functions as callbacks (event handlers) in JavaScript. Anonymous functions are just functions that aren't bound to a name and are instantiated when they are called and garbage collected shortly thereafter.

A simplified event-driven paradigm looks something like this:

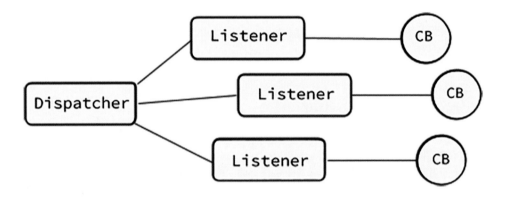

(An event can have multiple listeners, each with their own handler.)

Remember all those potatoes in your inventory? Let's write a little function that listens for every time a SpigotMC PlayerItemConsumeEvent is dispatched. We're going to handle that event with an anonymous function. We can do anything we want in that function, so why don't we take a look at the sounds module and play a sound?

# Instructions

Thankfully, ScriptCraft has a really good module for handling events. Let's import that at the top of our {your name}-exercises.js file, and while we're at it, we can import the sounds module too.

```
var events = require('events');
var sounds = require('sounds');
```

You know the drill by now: we'll start by adding a function to our exercises called functionAnonymous. Now we need to add a handler to the "eat" event, which gets dispatched every time the player eats something. Luckily, the ScriptCraft events module is straightforward. Every SpigotMC event has a camel-cased version in ScriptCraft. Adding a handler for the eat event is as simple as

```
events.playerItemConsume(function(event) {
        // do something
});
```

That's pretty short! Essentially what we're doing here is registering a handler for the eat event—that handler is in the form of an anonymous function that takes the event as a parameter. Depending on the SpigotMC event type here: https://hub.spigotmc.org/javadocs/spigot/org/bukkit/event/Event.html, the event we're given in our anonymous function may have different properties. For instance, if we attach a handler to a PlayerItemConsumeEvent, the event instance has a method called getItem, which will allow us to inspect the item we're consuming. For instance, if baked potatoes give our character some gastrointestinal distress, we can make him burp—but we don't want to play that sound every time he or she consumes an item—only when a baked potato is consumed:

```
events.playerItemConsume(function(event) {
        if (event.getItem().getType() === items.bakedPotato()) {
                // give me gas
        }
});
```

Okay, we're almost there. The sounds module works a lot like the events module—all of the possible sounds found at https://hub.spigotmc.org/javadocs/spigot/org/bukkit/Sound.html can be played by calling their camel-cased equivalent. To play a burp sound, all we need to do is call a method with ENTITY_PLAYER _BURP in camel case:

```
sounds.entityPlayerBurp(); // gross
```
Putting it all together:
```
events.playerItemConsume(function(event) {
        if (event.getItem().getType() === items.bakedPotato()) {
                sounds.entityPlayerBurp();
        }
});
```

Okay, now eat one of those many baked potatoes by selecting them in your inventory and holding down the right mouse button. Excuse you!

Now you can try to register for different events and play different sounds based on the above links. Try your hand at looking up a Java Enum or class name on your own and listen to a new event or play a different sound!

# Handling Player Interaction

 1  25–30 minutes  Atom or your favorite IDE/text editor

## Activity Overview

We have a couple more function-related activities before we move on to some object-oriented programming. Woo hoo! We've covered events, which is one of the main ways we can deal with player interaction and input. Another way you can handle user input in ScriptCraft is by using the signs module, which lets us create interactive signs and use event-driven programming and anonymous functions to alter the world in some way. For this one, we'll play around with the items module a bit more and let players select items by interacting with the sign.

## Instructions

First, let's import the signs module at the top of our file:

```
var signs = require('signs');
```

If you've been listening to me, you know I've been naming all of our functions here in exercises. But now it's your turn! See if you can come up with a function name that is both clear and concise. I'll call mine interactiveSign.

The signs module is pretty interesting. Using the signs.menu static method, you can turn any sign in the game into an interactive menu. The method takes three parameters: a label for the sign, an array of choices (these must be strings), and a callback function that is called every time a user interacts with the sign. The signs.menu method then returns a function that we must then pass the current sign to in order to make it interactive.

Let's start with our choices array:

```
var choices = ['Shovel', 'Pickaxe', 'Hoe'];
```

We can then use an anonymous function for our callback, and store the resulting function in a variable, like so:

```
var convertToToolMenu = signs.menu('Tools',
    choices,
    function(event) {
        // do something with the event
    }
);
```

The function stored in convertToToolMenu takes a sign as a parameter and turns it into an interactive menu. But come on! How do we get the sign?

We need to pass a player argument to our function, and with that player information, we can use another static method called signs.getTargetedBy, which takes a CraftPlayer object as an argument. From there, it figures out if the player is currently targeting a sign—and if so, returns it. We need to check for the sign—if there is one, we'll call our convertToToolMenu function.

```
var sign = signs.getTargetedBy(player);
// returns null if there's no sign—told you it was a convention!
if (sign !== null) {
    convertToToolMenu(sign);
}
/* could put an echo here to let the player know they need to target
a sign for this to work. */
```

Now, in order to run the function, we can place a sign by calling the global signpost function, passing our self variable in as a parameter for the location:

```
signpost(self);
```

This should place a signpost right in front of you, or at least near you. For now, it just says CraftPlayer. If you target it, and call exercises.interactiveSign(self), you should see the text change to this:

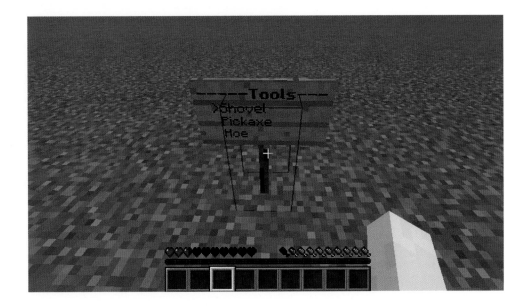

Great! You should also be able to cycle through it. But wait—it doesn't do anything yet. Now we can set up our event handling callback to actually give the desired tool to the player.

Because the choices array can only take strings, we need to create a second array with all of the item values in it. As long as the items have indices that correspond to the labels in the choices array, we can select the right ones.

```
var choices = ['Shovel', 'Pickaxe', 'Hoe'];
var values = [items.goldSpade(1), items.goldPickaxe(1), items.goldHoe(1)];
```

The event that gets passed to our anonymous function has a handy property called number, which will give us the current index that the user is on. Now all we have to do is recycle our technique for dropping items and we're home free!

```javascript
interactiveSign: function(player) {
    var world = player.world;
    var location = player.location;
    var choices = ['Shovel', 'Pickaxe', 'Hoe'];
    var values = [ items.goldSpade(1), items.goldPickaxe(1),
        items.goldHoe(1) ];
    var convertToToolMenu = signs.menu('Tools',
        choices,
        function(event) {
            world.dropItem(location, values[event.number]);
        }
);
var sign = signs.getTargetedBy(player);
if (sign !== null) {
    convertToToolMenu(sign);
    }
}
```

# Your Own Function!

 1  25–30 minutes  Atom or your favorite IDE/text editor

## Activity Overview

It's time for you to create your own function in the exercises object. Everything we've covered so far should give you the tools you need to execute it!

## Instructions

By using previous examples, as well as the ScriptCraft API documentation, create a function that does all of the following:

- Listens to one of the events listed here: https://github.com /walterhiggins/ScriptCraft/blob/master/docs/API-Reference .md#events-helper-module-spigotmc-version.
- Uses both an anonymous function and a named function, either of which must take at least one argument and return something.
- Calls one of the other functions or objects we've used (drone, items module, sounds module, etc).

You're well on your way to writing your first awesome *Minecraft* mod! At this point, we've almost completely covered the core concepts of programming in JavaScript. It seems like just yesterday we were typing "hello, world!" Are you beginning to see how a system like *Minecraft* works under the hood? There's really only one more thing we need to touch on before we can start actively modding, and that's object-oriented programming.

# Object-Oriented Programming (!)

Object-oriented programming is a very popular paradigm in the world of software development. JavaScript makes it pretty easy to understand, and thank goodness. In comparison to languages like Java or C++, JavaScript is much easier.

We're going to start slow—setting and getting properties—and then we'll move on to methods and prototypes. To put everything together and begin to understand not just how, but why we use object-oriented programming. We're going to write a tool that lets other programmers create custom crafting recipes. It'll have a constructor, properties, and methods.

# Me, My(self), and I

 1  10–15 minutes  **Atom or your favorite IDE/text editor**

## Activity Overview

Up to this point, we've really only been working with object-oriented programming from a distance. We've called a few methods and constructed a few instances (remember the drone?), but we haven't really done any object-oriented programming of our own. If you remember from way back in chapter one, an object is an instance of a class that has properties (data) and methods (functions that do something with the data). We're going to play around with some of the properties and methods on our self object, which is an instance of the CraftPlayer class.

## Instructions

A lot of this will likely be review for you, but review is really helpful! To access an object's property, we can use either the dot operator or its index:

```
echo(self, self.allowFlight);
>> false
```
**// or**
```
echo(self, self['allowFlight']);
```

A common pattern in object-oriented languages, especially Java, is the use of what are called getter and setter methods. These methods read (get) and write (set) an object's properties. Normally, you want other programmers to access object properties in a controlled way. In a language like Java, you can actually establish visibility rules for properties. In other words, you can make certain properties public and immutable by outside code.

This is a long-winded way of saying that JavaScript has no explicit concept of private properties, although there are ways for you to achieve them via scoping and closures. In most cases, you can just get and set properties like this:

```
self.allowFlight = true;
```
**// now you can fly!**

Methods aren't just used for getting and setting. You can also use them to perform functions that are tied to the class specifically. For instance, a player's chat method doesn't get or set anything, but it's something that is still tied to the player— that particular instance of the CraftPlayer class is sending the message:

```
self.chat("Hi everybody!");
>> <jromphf> Hi everybody!
```

The previous is an example of an instance method—it has to be called an instance of the class because it uses some instance properties—in this case it displays my username when I post the message. A static method is just like a function, only it's encapsulated by, or part of, a class. It doesn't use any instance properties, but its inclusion in the class makes sense because whatever job it performs does something related to the class. This is pretty complex stuff, but once we start making something, it should make more sense!

Go ahead and take a look at the player interface (which CraftPlayer implements) at https://hub.spigotmc.org/javadocs /bukkit/org/bukkit/entity/Player.html and try your hand at calling some of its methods.

# Real Classy

 1     10–15 minutes     Atom or your favorite IDE/text editor

## Activity Overview

We're going to get started with classes by writing a very basic one over the next few activities. We're going to come up with a new RecipeMaker class that makes it easier for us to create custom recipes. Most of the heavy lifting will be done by ScriptCraft's recipes module, which has a handy factory function to create recipes for us. Essentially, we'll be piecing together all of the necessary components that the function needs, as well as creating a couple of methods to handle adding and removing the recipe from the server. This is a concept that's known as encapsulation, where we combine data and functions into a class.

## Instructions

Now we're going to do something a little different. After our exports.exercises object, we're going to create our class. Creating classes in JavaScript is just like creating functions:

```
// exercises object is up here ^
var RecipeMaker = function() {

}
```

Notice how my variable is using Pascal case? That's because it's a class name, and we'd like to stick with the conventions of the language it's based on: Java. Now, to export that class, we add it to our exports object:

```
exports.RecipeMaker = RecipeMaker;
```

If we go into *Minecraft* and refresh, we can create an instance of our RecipeMaker class:

```
var rm = new RecipeMaker();
echo(self, rm);
>> [object Object]
```

By using the new operator, we end up calling the constructor function of our class, which takes in some arguments (we don't have any yet) and sets some instance properties (we don't have any of those either), returning a new object of type RecipeMaker.

# This and That

 1    10–15 minutes    Atom or your favorite IDE/text editor

## Activity Overview

Here, we're actually going to pass some arguments to our constructor and set some initial properties on our RecipeMaker instance. First, we need to think about what we need. The recipes.add static method requires the following:

- The material type that represents the result in our inventory
- The ingredients that go into crafting the recipe
- The shape of the ingredients in our crafting grid in order to yield the recipe

There are a couple of other things that we need in order to get everything ready before we call the recipes.add method:

- We need a name for the new item
- We need to add some sort of enchantment to make it special

These can all be considered properties that can be set using our constructor. Let's try it out.

# Instructions

Now we have our barebones class that does nothing:

```
var Recipemaker = function() {
}
```

Adding parameters to a constructor is exactly the same as adding them to a function:

```
var Recipemaker = function(name, enchantment, material,
ingredients, shape) {
    // but how do we set them??
}
```

To actually set the properties, we use the this keyword. This is common in most object-oriented languages—there's not too much to it, it just refers to the current class instance (or object). An example is the best way to show how keyword this works:

```
var RecipeMaker = function(name, enchantment, material,
ingredients, shape) {
    this.name = name;
    this.enchantment = enchantment;
    this.material = material;
    this.ingredients = ingredients;
    this.shape = shape;
}
```

Now, if we refresh ScriptCraft and pass dummy strings to our RecipeMaker constructor, we can see how the keyword this works.

```
var rm = new RecipeMaker("the name", "the enchantment", "the
material", "the ingredients", "the shape");
echo(self, rm.material);
>> "the material"
echo(self, rm.ingredients);
>> "the ingredients"
```

Try changing the constructor parameters and the object properties until you feel comfortable with what your new this keyword is doing. When you're ready, we'll make some methods!

# A Working Prototype

 1     10–15 minutes     Atom or your favorite IDE/text editor

## Activity Overview

Remember, instance methods are just functions that use some of the instance's properties. One way to determine whether a method is an instance method or a static method is if a this keyword is used anywhere in the method—if not, it's static, and can be called without calling a constructor and creating an object instance. There are a couple of different ways to create methods in JavaScript, but there's one way that I tend to favor. Let's try out some instance and static methods.

## Instructions

The easiest way to create an instance method is like this:

```
var RecipeMaker = function(name, enchantment, material,
ingredients, shape) {
```

```
        this.name = name;
        this.enchantment = enchantment;
        this.material = material;
        this.ingredients = ingredients;
        this.shape = shape;
        this.getMaterial = function() {
                return this.material;
        }
    }
//in Minecraft
var rm = new RecipeMaker("the name", "the enchantment", "the
material", "the ingredients", "the shape");
echo(self, rm.getMaterial());
>> "the material"
```

That was pretty easy. Do you see any problems with this
approach? Because this.getMaterial is being defined in the
constructor, it means that we're actually creating a new function
every time we construct a new RecipeMaker instance—not very
efficient at all.

Something that makes JavaScript different from a lot of other
major languages is that it uses something called prototypical
inheritance. Inheritance is an important concept in object-
oriented programming. Basically, classes can inherit properties
and methods from other classes.

In JavaScript, there aren't actual classes. Instead of classes,
it has something called prototypes. Every function in JavaScript
has a prototype, which stores methods and properties. When you
inherit from a specific prototype, you inherit all of those methods
and properties. Every object and function inherits methods and
properties from Object.prototype. If we want to add methods to
our RecipeMaker "class," we can add them in the prototype:

```
var RecipeMaker = function(name, enchantment, material,
ingredients, shape) {
```

```
    this.name = name;
    this.enchantment = enchantment;
    this.material = material;
    this.ingredients = ingredients;
    this.shape = shape;
}
RecipeMaker.prototype.getMaterial = function() {
    return this.material;
}
```

When you call it, it works exactly the same way as our other bit of code:

```
var rm = new RecipeMaker("the name", "the enchantment", "the
material", "the ingredients", "the shape");
echo(self, rm.getMaterial());
>> "the material"
```

Only this way, we don't have the inefficiency of creating a new function every time we construct a RecipeMaker instance. Similarly, it makes it easier to write static methods:

```
RecipeMaker.aStaticMethod = function() {
    echo(self, "I'm static");
}
```

Now we can call that without constructing an object like so:

```
RecipeMaker.aStaticMethod();
>> "I'm static"
```

See? Easy!

# Making the Recipe Maker: Part 1—Reflection

 1      15–20 minutes     ✖ Atom or your favorite IDE/text editor

## Activity Overview

Now that you're getting better at this, we're going to try to put a lot of the concepts into practice by actually making the recipe maker. We'll need to get into the SpigotMC and ScriptCraft guts a little bit more, but it should help you understand why we use object-oriented programming and why it's helpful.

Right now, we're actually going to check for the specific types of both the material and enchantment properties. Why would we do this? Well, in order for us to create our result, we absolutely have to have a material that is an ItemStack so we can add an enchantment to it. Similarly, the enchantment has to be an Enchantment—otherwise, it all falls apart! The process of looking at a class and getting some info on it is known as reflection. For instance, you would use reflection to check an object's type, or what methods it has.

## Instructions

We now have the three properties that we need in order to successfully make a recipe. Our first order of business is the creation of the item that you'll get from using this recipe. We're going to modify the material to make it special. Remember, the material that gets passed in needs to be an ItemStack! We should actually check to make sure it's an ItemStack instance, and if not, we throw out an error. Yes, we're going from causing errors in the interpreter to purposefully creating them! That's some major progress.

Let's create a method called buildResult. In our constructor, we should also create a this.result variable and set it to null. Why? So we can express our intentions that it hasn't been computed (or built) yet, but it soon will be!

```
var RecipeMaker = function(name, enchantment, material,
ingredients, shape) {
    this.name = name;
    this.enchantment = enchantment;
    this.material = material;
    this.ingredients = ingredients;
    this.shape = shape;
    this.result = null;
    this.recipe = null;
}
RecipeMaker.prototype.buildResult = function() {
// Do some building
}
```

Pretty simple. Let's put our check in there to make sure we have an ItemStack instance. If we get this out of the way first, we can avoid other errors down the line.

For the sake of clarity and convenience, I'm going to store the ItemStack type in a static property that is shared across all instances:

```
RecipeMaker.ITEM_STACK_CLASS = Java.type('org.bukkit.
inventory.ItemStack').class;
```

Now, in our buildResult method:

```
RecipeMaker.prototype.buildResult = function() {
    if (this.material.class !== RecipeMaker.ITEM_STACK_CLASS) {
        throw new Error("Material must be of type " + RecipeMaker.
        ITEM_STACK_CLASS);
    }
}
```

Now, if the user adds the wrong material (like a string instead of an ItemStack), they'll get a helpful error message. Now we need to do something similar for the enchantment. The enchantment class is found in the package "org.bukkit .enchantments.Enchantment"—do you think you can create the mechanism for checking that the user has passed in an instance of the class Enchantment?

# Making the Recipe Maker: Part 2— Manipulating Object Properties

 1     30–45 minutes     Atom or your favorite IDE/text editor

## Activity Overview

Now that we've ensured that our material is an ItemStack and our enchantment is an Enchantment, we can go ahead and modify the material's properties and add the enchantment to it. Once we're done with that, we'll write a couple of methods to add and remove the recipe from the server!

## Instructions

By now, we should have something that looks like this:

```
var RecipeMaker = function(name, enchantment, material,
ingredients, shape) {
  this.name = name;
  this.enchantment = enchantment;
  this.material = material;
  this.ingredients = ingredients;
  this.shape = shape;
  this.result = null;
```

```
    this.recipe = null;
  }
 RecipeMaker.ITEM_STACK_CLASS = Java.type('org.bukkit.
 inventory.ItemStack').class;
   RecipeMaker.ENCHANTMENT_CLASS = Java.type('org.bukkit.
 enchantments.Enchantment').class;
   RecipeMaker.prototype.buildResult = function() {
    if (this.material.class !== RecipeMaker.ITEM_STACK_CLASS) {
        throw new Error("Material must be of type " +
      RecipeMaker.ITEM_STACK_CLASS);
    }
    if (this.enchantment.class !== RecipeMaker.ENCHANTMENT_
 CLASS) {
        throw new Error("Enchantment must be of type " +
      RecipeMaker.ENCHANTMENT_CLASS);
    }
  }
```

We can now do some work to build the item that is produced
by our recipe. We're going to assign it the name and enchantment
that the user provides. Here's our buildResult method now:

```
  RecipeMaker.prototype.buildResult = function() {
    if (this.material.class !== RecipeMaker.ITEM_STACK_CLASS) {
        throw new Error("Material must be of type " +
      RecipeMaker.ITEM_STACK_CLASS);
    }
    if (this.enchantment.class !== RecipeMaker.ENCHANTMENT_
 CLASS) {
        throw new Error("Enchantment must be of type " +
      RecipeMaker.ENCHANTMENT_CLASS);
    }
 // we're actually going to clone our material so we don't mess with
 it—we can easily build new results with it by calling this
 method again
```

```
this.result = this.material.clone();
// get the item's metadata
var meta = this.result.getItemMeta();
// set its display name to the provided name
meta.setDisplayName(this.name);
// replace the item's metadata with the new metadata
this.result.setItemMeta(meta);
}
```

Now this is where things are going to get a little tricky. If we want to set the item's enchantment, not only do we need the enchantment itself, that is, DAMAGE_ALL, which increases damage to all of the targets, we also need the level to set it at. There are a few ways to handle this. Can you think of any?

Well, we could go back and modify our constructor so that we pass in the level, too, but that would give us a lot of arguments. We could also make users pass in an object with "enchantment" and "level" properties. Another solution is to remove the enchantment as a property and just add "enchantment" and "level" as parameters to our buildResult method. This isn't a bad idea because then this would allow for the user to be able to swap enchantments on the resulting item. Here's our new and improved buildResult method:

```
RecipeMaker.prototype.buildResult = function(enchantment, level) {
    if (this.material.class !== RecipeMaker.ITEM_STACK_CLASS) {
        throw new Error("Material must be of type " +
        RecipeMaker.ITEM_STACK_CLASS);
    }
// notice we're no longer using 'this' because there's no
enchantment property
    if (enchantment.class !== RecipeMaker.ENCHANTMENT_
CLASS) {
        throw new Error("Enchantment must be of type " +
        RecipeMaker.ENCHANTMENT_CLASS);
    }
```

```
    // we're actually going to clone our material so we don't mess
    with it
    this.result = this.material.clone();
    // get the item's metadata
    var meta = this.result.getItemMeta();
    // set its display name to the provided name
    meta.setDisplayName(this.name);
    // replace the item's metadata with the new metadata
    this.result.setItemMeta(meta);
    // now all we have to do is add the enchantment
    this.result.addEnchantment(enchantment, level);
}
```

We did quite a bit there! We're on a roll, so we might as well finish the job.

Let's write another method that calls recipes.add and makes the recipe:

```
RecipeMaker.prototype.makeRecipe = function() {
if (this.result === null) {
    throw new Error('Must call the buildResult method before
 you can make the recipe!');
}
this.recipe = {
result: this.result,
ingredients: this.ingredients, // an object with items
shape: this.shape, // the shape represents the positions of the
items in the rows on the workbench
}
var result = recipes.add(this.recipe);
/* recipes.add returns a ShapedRecipe or undefined. We're
going to make it more consistent with the rest of our code—if we
don't get a result, we return null */
if (result !== undefined) {
    return result;
```

```
    }
    return null;
}
```

When we actually write a function to test this class in the next activity, I'll explain what our ingredients and our shape properties look like. Now, all we have to do is write a couple of methods to add and remove the recipe from the SpigotMC server.

```
RecipeMaker.prototype.add = function() {
    server.addRecipe(this.recipe);
}
RecipeMaker.prototype.remove = function() {
    server.removeRemove(this.recipe);
}
```

# Making the Recipe Maker: Part 3—Testing Our Work

 1    35–45 minutes    Atom or your favorite IDE/text editor

## Activity Overview

We're almost there! All that's left is to write a quick function to test our RecipeMaker and make sure it's working—if it passes, we'll echo a success message. If it fails, we'll log an error. We'll also stock our inventory with the proper items we need to make our Emerald Sword so we can be 100 percent sure everything is working. Although this is pretty simple, it's usually a pretty great idea to set up some automated tests to make sure your code works as expected.

## Instructions

Okay, let's create another function called testRecipeMaker:

```
exports.testRecipeMaker = function() {
    // our tests go here
```

```
}
```

Now, we just need to call our RecipeMaker constructor. First, we'll start with our ingredients object:

```
exports.testRecipeMaker = function() {
// emerald sword from https://www.spigotmc.org/wiki/recipe
-example
  var ingredients = {
  E: items.emerald(1),
  S: items.stick(1),
  }
}
```

So, the ingredients are pretty straightforward. According to the SpigotMC example, they're using a stick and an emerald to make an emerald sword. The key, or property, can be anything, although the SpigotMC convention is to use the uppercase version of the first letter of the item—for example, E(merald) and S(tick).

Next is the shape, which is a little more confusing. The shape is an array that represents the rows in the crafting grid in your inventory. Let's say we want this recipe to be crafted on the normal 2x2 crafting grid, and the player just needs to add an emerald to one row and a stick to another, like this:

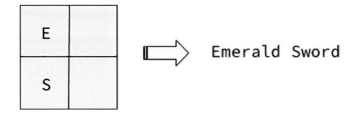

Our array would look like this ["E", "S", " "], where "E" represents the first row, and "S" represents the second row. The empty characters " " are just there to tell SpigotMC to ignore the third row and columns (2x2 instead of 3x3). If we wanted to restrict the item to a 3x3 grid, we'd do something like this:

| E | E | S |
|---|---|---|
| S | E | E |
| E | E | E |

⟹ Emerald Sword

And our "shape" array would look like this: ["EES", "SEE", "EEE"].

Every element in the array corresponds to a row in the crafting grid. Every character in each string corresponds to a column in that row. Let's make an easy one for now:

**var** shape = ["EE", "SS", " "];

This means the user will have to have one row of 2 emeralds and one row of 2 sticks to craft the emerald sword, like this:

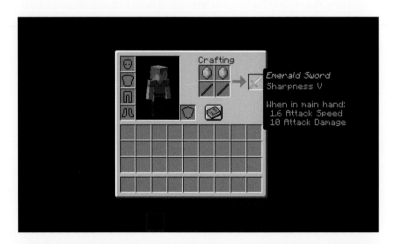

Now we can construct our RecipeMaker object. Remember, the parameters are name, material, ingredients, shape:

```
var rm = new RecipeMaker("Emerald Sword", items.
diamondSword(1), ingredients, shape);
```

We're using items.diamondSword(1) for the graphical representation of our sword since we can't create custom graphics for it (bummer). When users see it in their inventory and hold it in their hand, it'll be a diamond sword—but it'll be called an emerald sword and will be able to do more damage.

With that out of the way, we need to make the result. To do that, we just have to call the buildResult method with an enchantment and a level:

```
var enchantment = Java.type('org.bukkit.enchantments.
Enchantment').DAMAGE_ALL;
```

All of the available enchantments are here: https://hub
.spigotmc.org/javadocs/spigot/org/bukkit/enchantments
/Enchantment.html. Now all we need to do is build it and add it!

```
rm.buildResult(enchantment.DAMAGE_ALL, 5);
rm.makeRecipe();
var res = rm.add();
```

Now we can check to see if we got a result, or null:

```
if (res !== null) {
 echo(self, "RecipeMaker: Recipe Successfully Added!");
} else {
 echo(self, "RecipeMaker: Failed to Add Recipe!");
}
```

For good measure, let's give ourselves the items we need to actually craft it:

```
inventory(self)
.add(items.emerald(2))
.add(items.stick(2));
```

Now we should be able to make one of these!

Here is our RecipeMaker in its entirety. You should be proud—I sure am!

```
var RecipeMaker = function(name, material, ingredients, shape)
{
    this.name = name;
    this.material = material;
    this.ingredients = ingredients;
    this.shape = shape;
    this.result = null;
    this.recipe = null;
}

RecipeMaker.ITEM_STACK_CLASS = Java.type('org.bukkit
```

```
.inventory.ItemStack').class;
    RecipeMaker.ENCHANTMENT_CLASS = Java.type('org.bukkit
.enchantments.EnchantmentWrapper').class;

    RecipeMaker.prototype.buildResult = function(enchantment,
level) {
    if (this.material.class !== RecipeMaker.ITEM_STACK_CLASS) {
        throw new Error("Material must be of type " + RecipeMaker
    .ITEM_STACK_CLASS);
    }

    if (enchantment.class !== RecipeMaker.ENCHANTMENT
_CLASS) {
        throw new Error("Enchantment must be of type " +
    RecipeMaker.ENCHANTMENT_CLASS);
    }
 // we're actually going to clone our material so we don't mess
with it
    this.result = this.material.clone();
    // get the item's metadata
    var meta = this.result.getItemMeta();
    // set its display name to the provided name
    meta.setDisplayName(this.name);
    // replace the item's metadata with the new metadata
    this.result.setItemMeta(meta);
    this.result.addEnchantment(enchantment, level);
    }

    RecipeMaker.prototype.makeRecipe = function() {
    if (this.result === null) {
        throw new Error('Must call the buildResult method before
    you can make the recipe!');
    }
    this.recipe = {
    result: this.result,
```

```
ingredients: this.ingredients, // an object with items
shape: this.shape, // the shape represents the positions of the items
in the rows on the workbench
    }
  }

  RecipeMaker.prototype.add = function() {
   return recipes.add(this.recipe);
  }

  RecipeMaker.prototype.remove = function() {
   recipes.remove(this.recipe);
  }

  exports.testRecipeMaker = function() {
// emerald sword from https://www.spigotmc.org/wiki/recipe
-example
    var ingredients = {
    E: items.emerald(1),
    S: items.stick(1),
    }
// two rows on the 2x2 craft bench
    var shape = ["EE", "SS", " "];
    var rm = new RecipeMaker('Emerald Sword', items.
diamondSword(1), ingredients, shape);
    var enchantment = Java.type('org.bukkit.enchantments.
Enchantment').DAMAGE_ALL;
    rm.buildResult(enchantment.DAMAGE_ALL, 5);
    rm.makeRecipe();
    var res = rm.add();
    if (res !== null) {
    echo(self, "RecipeMaker: Recipe Successfully Added!");
    inventory(self)
    .add(items.emerald(2))
    .add(items.stick(2));
```

```
  } else {
  echo(self, "RecipeMaker: Failed to Add Recipe!");
  }
}

exports.RecipeMaker = RecipeMaker;
```

You just made it through a massive crash course on programming in JavaScript. You're definitely ready to start working on your awesome *Minecraft* mod now. Actually, you've pretty much made one already with the RecipeMaker! And it was pretty painless, wasn't it?

The next step will be trying to figure out all the moving parts of our Cellar Dweller mod. All of the next chapter is going help you put the mod together. You'll learn about some new programming techniques, but a lot of the new developments you'll be making will be conceptual ones. You'll learn about different patterns, how objects interact, how you can document your code, and how you can share your work with the world. By the end, you'll have a functioning dungeon crawler mod. Now that's something you can really be proud of!

# Chapter Three

# PUTTING IT ALL TOGETHER

T ime to take everything we learned in the last chapter and put it all together into a fully interactive mod! There are still a lot of ScriptCraft tools that we can work with to make it happen. We're going to build a dungeon crawler mod, which constructs random dungeons and fills them with monsters and loot—all on the fly! To do that, you're going to have to learn more about advanced programming techniques and paradigms, such as functional programming, event-driven programming, and persistence. Then, you'll learn how to properly document your mod so that other developers can work with it. And finally, I'm going to help you discover ways to distribute your brand-new mod to people (like your friends) who want to try it! Every activity in this chapter will require a computer, a copy of *Minecraft: Java Edition*, the SpigotMC Server with ScriptCraft installed, and Atom or your favorite IDE/text editor unless otherwise noted.

## Setup and Planning

Before you can start making up your awesome mod, let's take some time to think this out and plan ahead. We'll start off by setting up modules in ScriptCraft, which is a bit different from setting up plugins. We'll also sketch out the design of our mod and look into some of the underlying libraries that are going to power it. We'll end with a crash course in 3D graphics and delve a bit further into how the drone object works.

# The Mod Squad

 1  🕐 10–15 minutes

## Activity Overview

It's finally time for us to get started on our mod! Before we get too deep into it, we have to distinguish between how ScriptCraft handles plugins and how it handles modules. For the record, we'll be writing a module, which does have some differences. We're also going to learn about how to download existing libraries and import them into our code. Once we're done with that, we can start planning our Cellar Dweller mod.

## Instructions

For starters, everything we've been working on so far has been located in ScriptCraft's plugins directory. In ScriptCraft, every function name or variable at the root level of every file in the plugins directory is loaded into the global namespace. Modules, by default, are not loaded into the global namespace. Ops are responsible for loading these manually via the require module.

So, for our dungeon project, which I'm calling Cellar Dweller (you can come up with a better name if you want), we're actually going to create a folder in the spigotmc/scriptcraft/modules directory. Create a new folder in {your-spigotmc-dir}/scriptcraft /modules called cellar-dweller.

From here, we're going to download a library that I've written that's full of smaller helper modules that will make the process of creating our mod much easier. For starters, let's download the drone-dungeon extension from https://github.com/jjromphf /scriptcraft-drone-dungeon. Now, all we have to do is extract the folder to {your-spigotmc-dir}/scriptcraft/modules.

- **On a Mac**: move the zip file to {your-spigotmc-dir}
  /scriptcraft/modules and double-click on it. Now you should
  have a folder called drone-dungeon.
- **On Windows:** right-click on the zip file and select Extract
  All. From there, you can either pick the directory to extract to
  ({your-spigotmc-dir}/scriptcraft/modules) or extract it to your
  downloads directory and move the folder to {your-spigotmc
  -dir}/scriptcraft/modules.

We're almost done with the setup. I just want to show you
how to import a local file, which is a little bit different from
importing one of the ScriptCraft modules that we're used to. Let's
go ahead and create a new file in our cellar-dweller folder called
index.js. An index.js file is the file that require looks in when we
attempt to load a module based on its folder name. Now, on the
first line of the file, let's require the drone-dungeon module:

```
var dungeon = require('../drone-dungeon');
```

Notice that "../" before the "drone-dungeon"? That means
that the module we want to import is one directory up from
the current directory we're working in. This is what we refer to
as a relative path, or relative import—meaning that the path we
specify is relative to our file. There's also something called an
absolute path, which refers to the full path to the module we're
trying to import (for example: Users/joshr/spigotmc/scriptcraft
/modules/drone-dungeon).

Next let's make an empty function for now and export it to
make sure everything is linked up.

```
var CellarDweller = function() {

}

module.exports = CellarDweller;
```

Now, if we try to import it in *Minecraft* ...

```
var CellarDweller = require('cellar-dweller');
```

If all goes according to plan, you should be ready to go!

# Modeling the Mod

 1    25–30 minutes    Paper, pencil

## Activity Overview

When dealing with larger projects—and a mod sure is a large project—it helps to draw out the components you're dealing with and try to make sense of how they work together. In software development, this practice is called modeling. Take my word for it: It really helps you to think about what you want your program/app/ piece of software to do. It also helps you with all the different ways you can achieve it. I find myself constantly consulting models and diagrams, especially when I'm trying to implement a complex system.

## Instructions

Even if you think your parents are super uncool, they may remember dungeon crawler games like *Gauntlet and Diablo* from back when they played video games. Ask them! The premise of dungeon crawlers is pretty simple: you explore a dark environment (usually a dungeon or a castle), fight a lot of monsters, and grab as much loot as you can.

Our Cellar Dweller mod takes inspiration from something called a rogue-like, which is a dungeon-crawler style game with randomly generated—or procedural—levels. I've already created the library that we're going to use to handle this procedural part and lay out the rooms (no need to thank me ... but you can if you want), but it's up to you to actually make them interesting and fun.

So, what kinds of things do we need to make this fun? Well, we need:

- Monsters to battle—these should be randomly spawned.
- Loot to grab—this should also be randomly spawned.
- A way to keep track of how much loot has been collected and how many enemies a player has defeated.
- A mechanism to place dungeons and keep track of how many monsters and loot are in them at any given time.
- A way to save a player's progress.

It may seem like a lot, but we actually already have all of the pieces. We just need to put them together—which is where our drawing comes in.

Start off with something like this:

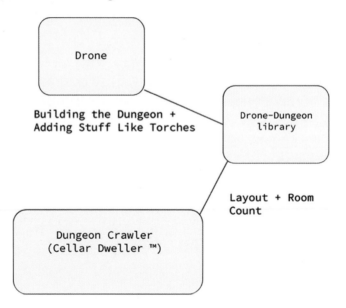

We have our Cellar Dweller mod, which uses my Drone-Dungeon library to build the rooms—it relies on ScriptCraft's drone module to do all the actual building, as well as placing stuff like doors and torches. Let's think about what else we need:

- An event system to keep track of player interactions (i.e., jromphf picked up a diamond sword).
- A module to deal with persistence, or saving player status.
- A module for randomly spawning enemies.
- A module for randomly spawning loot.

Want to try your hand at drawing your own diagram like the one above and adding those extra pieces to the puzzle? I hope so! To help you out, though, I've already written the event system for us to work with, and ScriptCraft has a built-in persistence and a spawn module. Let's see how you make out with putting these together!

Here's what my final diagram looks like:

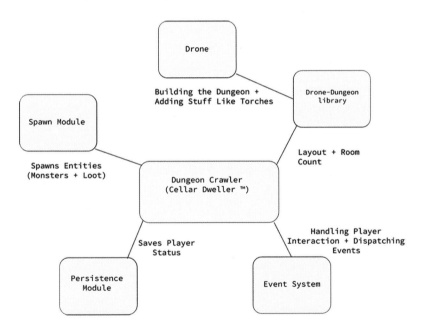

# Getting Situated

  1  ⏱ 20–25 minutes

## Activity Overview

Now that there's a decent map of how the mod is going to function, you can start thinking about how each of the individual parts work. Let's get started by delving a little bit deeper into the drone, which the Drone-Dungeon library uses extensively.

## Instructions

If you want to construct anything in the *Minecraft* world, you'll have to get a grasp on working in 3D space. Because *Minecraft* works in three dimensions, we're dealing with three axes (and not the kind used in battle): *x*, *y*, and *z*.

In *Minecraft*, the axes are as follows:

- The *x* axis moves from west to east (left to right)
- The *y* axis moves up and down
- The *z* axis moves from north to south (forward and backward)

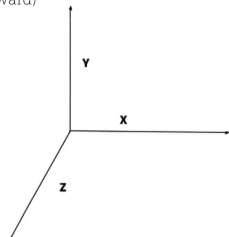

Just to make sure, let's echo our own location:

```
echo(self, self.location)
>> Location{...(location stuff)}
```

See the $x$, $y$, and $z$ there? That's what we're going to take advantage of when we use the drone.

Time to create a drone object at our location:

```
var drone = new Drone(self);
```

The drone has $x$, $y$, $z$, and *dir* (short for direction) properties. If we want to, we can set a checkpoint to save our drone's position and move back to it whenever we want.

```
drone.chkpt('start');
```

This will set its "start" checkpoint to the current location.

Now, the way the drone works is a little confusing. The drone has the following movement methods:

- up
- down
- left
- right
- fwd
- back

The drone moves in units of a single block, but you can pass $n$ number of blocks to any of the methods, and it will move that many blocks in that direction. For example, drone.up(5) will move 5 blocks up (in the $y$ direction).

In terms of the $x$ and $z$ axes, the drone moves relative to the direction it's facing:

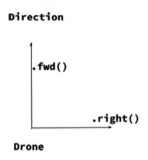

So let's say you're facing north. If you call the drone's .right() method, you'll move east along the *x* axis. If the drone is facing south, you'll move west along the *x* axis. This is really useful if we're moving only in object space, which is relative to the object that the drone is building. World space, on the other hand, refers to that object's position within the larger world—that is, the wide world of *Minecraft*.

When you move the drone to a location using its move method, you're moving relative to world space. This means you need to pass either a Location object to it, or the individual *x*, *y*, *z*, and *dir* variables. (The move method can also take a string value, which specifies a checkpoint.)

The drone can construct a lot of prefabricated objects, but we're going to try some lower-level stuff. In order to make boxes, the drone has a couple of methods. The box() method takes 4 parameters: the block material you're building with, as well as the width (*x*), height (*y*), and depth (*z*) you want the structure to be.

```
// here's a 1x2x3 stone box
drone.box(blocks.stone, 1, 2, 3);
```

You can also make a box with the inside hollowed out using boxa:

```
drone.boxa(blocks.stone, 1, 2, 3);
```

All right, that was pretty easy! Now you should be a box pro. Now challenge yourself by making the following boxes:

- A solid box of w=8, h=3, d=5
- Move forward 5 blocks and make a hollow oak box of h=10, w=10, d=4
- Move up 2 blocks and make a solid brick box of d=10, w=6, h=1
- Move left 10 blocks and make a hollow box of w=3, h=2, d=12
- Move back to your "start" checkpoint and make a glowstone box that's 1x1x1
- Move to any arbitrary *x*, *y*, *z*, *dir* location and make a redstone box of w=10, d=3, h=12

# Drone-Dungeon

All right, now that we know what we want to do—and how the drone object works a bit better—we can start laying some dungeons down! We'll use the Drone-Dungeon library that I wrote to do all the heavy lifting. We'll touch on binary space partitioning, which is the technique used to generate the randomly placed rooms within the dungeon. We'll also look at the many options available in the Drone-Dungeon library and will learn about how to set default options using ternary operators.

# BSP and Me

 1  15–20 minutes

## Activity Overview

Now that you know a bit more about how the drone moves, it's time to explore the Drone-Dungeon module. Ever heard of binary space partitioning? If not, we're going to go through what it is and how it's used to generate our dungeon's layouts, and then we're going drop some dungeon layouts on our map.

## Instructions

Although it's a little advanced for a beginner, we're going to briefly touch on binary space partitioning (BSP), which is the algorithm I used to make our random dungeon layout. It's one of the simplest and most common ways to generate a random floor plan for a dungeon.

With BSP, we can divide a rectangle (the space) up into smaller subsections (partitioning) by twos (binary). We recursively create partitions, meaning we make partitions within the partitions, one smaller than the next, and split the room up until we've gone through a set number of iterations (loops). We can then create a randomly sized rectangle in each one of those partitions, which becomes our room. Ultimately, we end up with a 2D—as opposed to 3D—layout like this one:

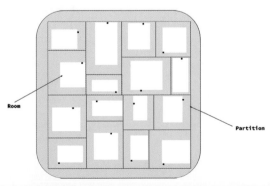

As you can see, all the smaller rectangles with black dots on them (the dots are randomly positioned doors) are different enough in size and have enough space around them that we can move around pretty freely. (You don't really need to know what BSP is, or how it works; I just wanted to keep you in the loop about some of the stuff going on behind the scenes.)

This is what a random layout looks like in 3D, without any walls, ceiling, or floors:

The Drone-Dungeon module takes a number of parameters:

1. The width of the dungeon (the *x* axis of the floor plan)
2. The height (depth) of the dungeon (the *y* axis of the floor plan)
3. The location, in world space (*x, y, z, dir*) of where we want to put our dungeon
4. Optional parameters that we'll explore in the next activity

Let's just make a dungeon and see what happens. We're going to use a different technique to import our Drone-Dungeon module. Because the Drone-Dungeon module is a function that extends—or adds functionality—to the drone object, we can actually require it and call it all in one line:

```
var dungeon = require('drone-dungeon')();
```

What this ends up doing is making a new method available on a drone instance, called dungeon, which we can then call to make a, well, dungeon.

```
var drone = require('Drone');
var dungeon = require('drone-dungeon')();
//we'll make one with the default options at our current location
drone.dungeon(50, 50, {}, self.location);
```

Now you've got your very own dungeon layout. It's not much right now, but soon you'll be populating it with a bunch of crazy monsters. Walk in and take a look around!

# Dungeon Master

 1   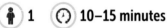 10–15 minutes

## Activity Overview

We're going to take a closer look at the options built into the Drone-Dungeon library to further customize our layouts. We'll be able to use these options in our Cellar Dweller mod to increase the complexity and difficulty of the dungeon layouts. Because, after all, who wants a boring dungeon?

# Instructions

Below are the properties available for the options object passed to the Drone.dungeon function:

- **iterations:** the number of iterations that we go through to split up the layout. The more iterations, the more rooms there will be. If the width and height of our dungeon is too small, this will end up in a StackOverflowError (we run out of memory)—so proceed with caution!
- **lightMode:** how dark or how bright our dungeon will be. Options are dark (no lights), dim, medium, and bright. You can either use the DungeonMaker.LIGHTMODES object or pass in a number from 0 to 4.
- **blockType:** The type of blocks used to build the dungeon and its rooms. Any valid block type from the blocks module will work.
- **depth:** The depth of the structure—this is kind of confusing, but it corresponds to the *y* axis in the *Minecraft* world. In other words, it's the height of the ceiling.
- **doorType:** The type of door to be placed on each one of the rooms. Options are door (the normal wooden door), door2 (wooden double doors), iron (an iron door), door2_iron (iron double doors), or random. You can use the DungeonMaker. DOORTYPES object for this.
- **isTopFloor:** An internal option that specifies whether or not the floor is the top floor (we don't build any ladders if it is).

So, try it out! Create an options object and see if you can get your dungeon going!

# Ternary to the Rescue!

 1  ⏱ 20–25 minutes

## Activity Overview

Now we're going to learn about the ternary operator, which is a very handy way of doing inline (all in one line) conditional statements. Who needs all of those curly brackets anyways? Ternary operators are particularly useful if you need to
a) check if several properties in an object are set, and
b) find out what to do if those properties aren't set.
We're going to go ahead and set up some default options for our Cellar Dweller mod using ternary operators instead of IF statements or switch cases.

## Instructions

Right now, our Cellar Dweller mod looks like this:

```
var CellarDweller = function() {

}
```

We know we want the user to be able to set the location, as well as the size of the dungeon, and we'll want to pass in an options object that we will then send on down to the Drone .dungeon function, along with the location, width, and height:

```
var CellarDweller = function(location, w, h, options) {

}
```

There you have it! Now let's set the properties we know must be present. If we don't have a location, width, or height, we can also throw an error. But we'll do that later.

```
var CellarDweller = function(location, w, h, options) {
    this.location = location;
    this.w = w;
    this.h = h;
    this.options = options;
}
```

Now, what to do with those options? We don't want to pass them down to our Drone.dungeon function if they're wrong! This is where the ternary operator comes in. It looks like this: (condition) ? what to do if condition is true : what to do if it's false.

And to translate that into JavaScript:

```
var myTernary = (true === false) ? 1 : 0;
echo(self, myTernary);
>> 0
```

Get it? It's just like a condensed IF statement and is the equivalent of writing this:

```
var myTernary;
if (true === false) {
    myTernary = 1;
} else {
    myTernary = 0;
}
```

That's a lot longer! This is how we can use it in our constructor:

```
var CellarDweller = function(location, w, h, options) {
    this.location = location;
    this.w = w;
```

```
        this.h = h;
        this.options = options;
        this.nFloors = (options.nFloors !== undefined) ? options.
        nFloors : 1;
    }
```

What we're doing here is creating our own "safe" settings to pass down to Drone.dungeon.

We should really set some defaults for width, location, and height, too. Can you set them using ternary operators just like I did with this.nFloors? Here are defaults you can use:

```
    this.location: self.location
    this.w: 50
    this.h: 50
    this.depth: 5
```
**\*\*Note: the depth property needs to be passed in via options just like nFloors.**

This way, we're 100 percent sure we're passing something usable down to Drone.dungeon. In the next activity, we'll actually go ahead and use a FOR loop to make some floors.

## Making Dungeons

Now that you've added some new tools (not to mention some new lingo) into your skillset, it's time to make some dungeons with randomly placed rooms. We'll write a method in our Cellar Dweller mod to place the rooms and add multiple floors to the dungeon. We'll store our rooms in a data structure so we can keep track of them and provide useful information to other developers using our mod. We'll conclude by exploring ways we can make our dungeons look more like dungeons, rather than boring stone boxes.

# Make Some Dungeons!

 1   15–20 minutes

## Activity Overview

Now we need to write a method that takes all of our Cellar Dweller properties and passes them on to Drone.dungeon. Drone.dungeon doesn't have any default way of handling multiple floors, so we're going to go ahead and add that functionality to our module to make our dungeons more interesting. Let's see if you remember how to do a FOR loop.

## Instructions

Let's write our first method in the CellarDweller mod:

```
CellarDweller.prototype.makeDungeons = function() {
    // good thing we have an nFloors property! And good
    thing you know how to write a FOR loop!
}
```

Okay, do you think you can put a FOR loop in that makeDungeons method based on our nFloors property? Once you do that, we can put some logic in there for actually making the floor.

Soon, you should have something like this:

```
CellarDweller.prototype.makeDungeons = function() {
    for(var i = 0; i < this.nFloors; i++) {
        // make floors
    }
}
```

Now for some floor action. The trick to making the floors is to move our drone up to the right position for each iteration. Because we're building up, the drone needs to move up the same amount as our depth for every iteration. There's also an extra two blocks on every ceiling to account for some hidden glowstone that works as an ambient light in the dungeon, so we need to take that into account, too.

```javascript
CellarDweller.prototype.makeDungeons = function() {
    for(var i = 0; i < this.nFloors; i++) {
        var currentLocation = {
            x: this.location.x,
            y: this.location.y + ((this.depth + 2) * i),
            z: this.location.z
        }
    }
}
```

See what we're doing there? The depth + 2 accounts for the depth of the room and the two ceiling blocks. We then multiply that by *i* and add it to the initial location. So, if our *y* location is 4, our depth is 5, and we have 3 floors:

*Y* location at first iteration: 4
*Y* location at second iteration: 11 (4 + (7 x 1))
*Y* location at third iteration: 18 (4 + (7 x 2))

Not bad! Now we just need to take care of a bit of housekeeping. We need to pass in an isTopFloor option to Drone .dungeon so that the ladders don't extend out past the ceiling. Unless you want ladders to nowhere. (Hint: You don't.)

How can we identify which floor is the top one? Well, it should be this.nFloors−1 (because we're initializing *i* to 0).

Kind of like our ternary operator, we can also write an inline condition that evaluates to true or false:

```javascript
var isTopFloor = i === this.nFloors−1;
```

This checks to see if *i* is at the top floor. Pretty clean! Okay, now all we have to do is instantiate a drone and pass the params to its dungeon method:

```
CellarDweller.prototype.makeDungeons = function() {
    for(var i = 0; i < this.nFloors; i++) {
        var currentLocation = {
            x: this.location.x,
            y: this.location.y + ((this.depth + 2) * i),
            z: this.location.z
        }
        this.options.isTopFloor = i === this.nFloors−1;
        var drone = new Drone(this.location);
        drone.dungeon(this.w, this.h, this.options,
            currentLocation);
    }
}
```

# Keeping Track of Our Rooms

 1  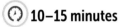 10–15 minutes

## Activity Overview

Now that we're generating the rooms, we'll need to come up with a mechanism for keeping track of them! This will be useful for detecting whether and where a player picks up an item in the dungeon.

## Instructions

The Drone-Dungeon module has a dungeons property, but it's a flat array, with each dungeon having a layout property that holds the rooms. Remember, all of the rooms are 2D layouts, too—so we'll have to do a bit of problem solving to get all the information we need. Creative problem solving is one of the most rewarding aspects of programming—let's see if we can do it.We should add a this.floors property to our constructor and initialize it to an empty array:

```
var CellarDweller = function(location, w, h, options) {
    this.location = location;
    this.w = w;
    this.h = h;
    this.options = options;
    this.nFloors = (options.nFloors !== undefined) ? options.
    nFloors : 1;
this.floors = [];
}
```

Now, in our makeDungeons method, we can push each floor's rooms onto the array. We should also keep track of the floor's width, height, and depth. In that case, we'll need an object with these properties:

Width, height, rooms, location

If you want to go ahead and try this yourself, I think you should! If not, look down below for one way to do it.

```
CellarDweller.prototype.makeDungeons = function() {
    for(var i = 0; i < this.nFloors; i++) {
        var currentLocation = {
                x: this.location.x,
                y: this.location.y + ((this.depth + 2) * i),
                z: this.location.z
        }
        this.options.isTopFloor = i === this.nFloors−1;
        var drone = new Drone(this.location);
        drone.dungeon(this.w, this.h, this.options,
        currentLocation);
        // one way to keep track of our rooms
```

```
            var floorInfo = {
                    rooms: drone.dungeons[0].layout.rooms,
                    w: this.w,
                    h: this.h,
                    location: currentLocation
            }
            this.floors.push(floorInfo);
        }
    }
```

# Our Dungeon—Fortified!

 1    10–15 minutes

## Activity Overview

The dungeons that Drone-Dungeon makes are not very exciting at all. They're also not underground! The reason for that is simple: we can only build as far down as our world goes. So, rather than messing with the configuration in SpigotMC, I decided to build up. I also looked it up on the internet—and it turns out not all dungeons are underground. So there!

Anyway, we're going to import the DungeonMaker submodule from Drone-Dungeon, which has a static method called fortify, which we can use to optionally build a fort around our dungeon to make it a little more pleasing to the eye.

## Instructions

We can import the DungeonMaker submodule like so:

```
// other requires up here ^
var DungeonMaker = require('drone-dungeon/dungeon-
maker');
```

Let's go ahead and create our own fortify method to prepare the data that gets sent down to DungeonMaker.fortify:

```
CellarDweller.prototype.fortify = function() {
 // prepare data here
}
```

DungeonMaker.fortify takes three parameters, based on the same parameters as Drone.fort:

1.  A location
2.  A width
3.  A height
4.  A depth

This should all be pretty easy, except for one thing: because we're dealing with floors, we need to calculate a total depth so we can get the height of the structure right. We should have enough information to do that. But where could we compute it?
I'm going to go ahead and put it in the constructor like so:

```
// Other options up here ^
this.totalDepth = this.nFloors * (this.depth + 2);
```

Pretty easy! The only weirdness is that we have to include + 2 to our depth because of that ceiling offset—otherwise, it's pretty standard!
Okay, now let's finish off the method:

```
CellarDweller.prototype.fortify = function() {
DungeonMaker.fortify(this.location, this.w, this.h, this.
totalDepth);
}
```

Nice and simple. We've essentially just made what's known as a wrapper, which is a layer that we "wrap" around existing code to allow for a simpler implementation and interface. We know what the parameters are for DungeonMaker.fortify, so why complicate things by making the user manually enter them? Now we've gone from 3 parameters to none! And check out our new, fortified dungeon—pretty ominous!

# Spawning

These dungeons are pretty lonely and—dare I say—boring. Let's put some stuff in them! We'll curate some sets of monsters and items that we can randomly place. This is the real meat-and-potatoes section of our mod. We'll work on a method for randomly selecting both monsters and items and come up with a way to randomly place them. Along the way, we'll dip our toes into asynchronous programming (it's harder to pronounce than it actually is, I promise) and learn about some of the more complex aspects of JavaScript.

# Entities "R" Us

 1  15–20 minutes

## Activity Overview

Now we should have enough information to be able to spawn some entities. Let's take a look and see how the entities module works alongside the spawn module. First, we'll try spawning some entities at locations and see what happens. Then, we'll see if we can start the building blocks of creating our spawnEntities and spawnItems methods.

## Instructions

The entities module works a lot like the items module does. It is a set of functions, each named after the corresponding entity found here: https://hub.spigotmc.org/javadocs/spigot/org/bukkit/entity /EntityType.html.

Each property name corresponds to a snake case version of the entities found above. Like the items module, it gives you the type of an entity—you're responsible for spawning it with the spawn module!

The spawn module takes an entity type as its first parameter and a location value as its second. To spawn a polar bear at your location, you would do something like this:

```
var entities = require('entities');
var spawn = require('spawn');
spawn(entities.polar_bear(), self.location);
```

You should be looking at a polar bear right now. Well, now we know how to do that. But unlike the items module, we don't have an ItemStack to work with—so we need to handle spawning multiple entities on our own. There are a few things we're going to have to account for if we want to do that. First, though, you should give spawning multiple entities a try! Try it with a FOR loop, a while loop, and a forEach. When you're ready, we'll move on to the next activity—where we'll come up with a way of selecting a random number of entities!

# Random Entities: Part 1— Difficulty Options

 1  15–20 minutes

## Activity Overview

So how are we going to populate our dungeon with monsters? For starters, we'll need to come up with some way of spawning a random number of enemies dispersed across all of our floors. We don't want to have them clumped up in certain areas. Similarly, we don't want a ton of enemies or too few.

My thought process would be that we could have some sort of minimum and maximum number of enemies based on a difficulty level chosen by the user. Also, the number of enemies should be proportional to the area of our dungeon, but unfortunately there's a pretty hard spawn limit imposed on the server.

## Instructions

We can add a static property to our mod, which means that it can be called without an instance and is the same across all instances. This static property will hold our different difficulty levels. If we have numbers as values, we can multiply them by the maximum allowed value.

```
// CellarDweller constructor is here ^
CellarDweller.DIFFICULTY = {
    easy: 0.25, // 1/4 of the max value
    medium: 0.5, // 1/2 of the max value
    difficult: 0.75, // 3/4 of the max value
    insane: 1 // the max value
}
```

Now all we have to do is look for a difficulty property in the options that the user passes in. We need to make sure that the property is actually defined—and if it is, we have to make sure it's actually a valid option. If not, we set this.difficulty to medium. How would you do it? Give it a try—and if you get stuck, check out my code:

```
var CellarDweller = function(location, w, h, options) {
    this.location = location;
    this.w = w;
    this.h = h;
    this.options = options;
    this.nFloors = (options.nFloors !== undefined) ? options.
    nFloors : 1;
    this.rooms = [];
    var difficulty = (options.difficulty !== undefined) ? options.
    difficulty : 'medium';
    var userDifficulty = CellarDweller.DIFFICULTY[difficulty];
    this.difficulty = (userDifficulty !== undefined) ?
    userDifficulty : CellarDweller.DIFFICULTY.medium;
}
```

This is starting to feel like a serious minigame with real options!

# Random Entities: Part 2— The Random Part

 1     15–20 minutes

## Activity Overview

Now that we've got an idea of how to set difficulty options, we can go ahead and start to write the method that will give us a random number of enemies to spawn based on the difficulty we set. Then, we can use that number in another method to actually spawn the monsters.

## Instructions

First off, let's write the method. We'll have to account for a few things:

1. We need to create a random number of enemies between our min and max values.
2. We need to figure out how to get those values—now we don't have to worry about crashing anything!

That first part should be easy. I have a utility function in Drone-Dungeon that can give us a random integer between two values. So up at the top of our index.js file:

**var** randomInt = **require**('drone-dungeon/utils').randomInt;

See how I imported that one? You can move through folders and files with require, which is really cool. I have a function called randomInt in a file called utils within the drone-dungeon folder that I was able to import.

With that out of the way, let's write the method:

```
CellarDweller.prototype.getNumberOfEntities = function() {
    // let's say that the max value is our difficulty value * our
    max value, and the min value is half that—how do we do it?
}
```

Now, how do we make sure we don't accidentally spawn more entities than the server is capable of handling? Thankfully, the world object has something that will help us: a method called getMonsterSpawnLimit. This returns the spawn limit per chunk in our world, not for the whole world itself. The chunk is the current part of the world that the player is located in.

Notice how things start to appear and disappear as you walk around the world? Those are all of the entities and objects associated with chunks. Computers can't handle everything in the world all at once, so entities and objects are loaded on a chunk-by-chunk basis. Okay, that was a pretty long-winded way of saying that we'll probably only be able to get about seventy monsters per dungeon.

Here's how we get our max value through code:

```
CellarDweller.prototype.getNumberOfEntities = function() {
    // let's say that the max value is our difficulty value * our
    max value, and the min value is half that—how do we do it?
    var world = self.world;
    var max = world.getMonsterSpawnLimit() * this.difficulty;
    var min = max / 2;
}
```

Now for the random part. The randomInt function is really simple. It just takes a min and max value and returns a random integer between them:

```
CellarDweller.prototype.getNumberOfEntities = function() {
    var world = self.world;
    var max = world.getMonsterSpawnLimit() * this.difficulty;
    var min = max / 2;
    return randomInt(min, max);
}
```

We have our random value that's guaranteed to be above 0 and less than whatever amount will cause lag on our server. Yay!

# Random Entities: Part 3— Curated Monsters

 1    15–20 minutes

## Activity Overview

The entities module is awesome, but it's too bad there isn't a module called monsters that could give us an array of monsters. To keep things fresh, we should probably also select random monsters to be spawned. We're going to have to find a way to get an array of monsters so we can use randomInt to randomly select them.

## Instructions

Can you create an array of only monsters that live in a static property, just like our CellarDweller.DIFFICULTY does? The list of all monsters can be found here in the SpigotMC documentation: https://hub.spigotmc.org/javadocs/spigot/org/bukkit/entity /Monster.html.

Look under All Known Subinterfaces—those class names are all the names of the monsters we need! Just in case you have trouble getting all of them, here they are:

Blaze, CaveSpider, Creeper, ElderGuardian, Enderman, Endermite, Evoker, Giant, Guardian, Husk, Illager, Illusioner, PigZombie, Silverfish, Skeleton, Spellcaster, Spider, Stray, Vex, Vindicator, Witch, Wither, WitherSkeleton, Zombie, ZombieVillager

Great! Remember, you'll have to find the correct ScriptCraft entity types in order for this to work—I'll get you started with the first one:

```
CellarDweller.MONSTERS = [
    entities.blaze(),
]
```

Think you can get the rest? Also, you can leave some out if they're too scary!

# Random Entities: Part 4— Picking a Monster

 1   10–15 minutes

## Activity Overview

Now that we have our curated list of monsters, all we have to do is write a method that will randomly select one from the array for us. Luckily, we can access values from an array by their index. Which happens to be an integer. That randomInt function sure is coming in handy!

## Instructions

Can you figure out this method on your own? Here's what it needs to do:

- It doesn't take any parameters.
- It needs to use randomInt to find a monster in our CellarDweller.MONSTERS array.
- The randomInt result cannot exceed the size (length) of the array or else we'll get an error.
- The randomInt cannot be less than 0.
- We need to return the result from the array.

That seems like a lot, but you already know how to do this! Take a look below for (one of) the answers.

```
CellarDweller.prototype.getRandomMonster = function() {
    var monsters = CellarDweller.MONSTERS; // don't want to
    keep typing that
    var index = randomInt(0, monsters.length-1); // because
    they're 0 indexed!
    return monsters[index];
}
```

# Random Entities: Part 5— Picking a Point

 1   10–15 minutes

## Activity Overview

We've gotten a lot done, but now we have to figure out how to pick a random point in our dungeon so that we can place enemies and loot. We don't want to be placing them all over the map! We're going to use an object that's part of the Drone-Dungeon utils called BoxInfo. It provides a really useful method called getRandomPoint, which returns a spigotMC Location object that works with the spawn module. All we have to do is construct the BoxInfo object from our location, w, and h properties.

Because we're building our dungeon in object space, BoxInfo needs to do some work to figure out where structure is lying in the world. You won't have to program this, but it might be worth it to know what's going on behind the scenes. Because the drone always moves like this

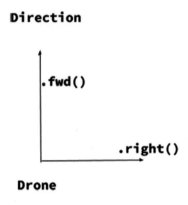

regardless of what direction it's facing, we end up with something like this:

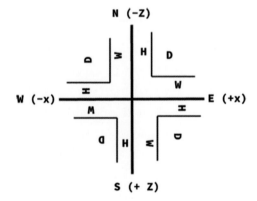

Where *D* is the dungeon, *H* is the height of our dungeon layout in 2D space, and *W* is the width. But depending on the direction that the drone was facing when we built the dungeon, we won't be able to work with the information we have. For instance, take the dungeon we built with the drone facing east. Typically, width moves along the *x* axis (horizontal), but as you can see here, it's actually our height. Or if we build facing north, our height is actually negative in world space.

What the BoxInfo object does is perform what's called a transformation: it transforms, or changes the positional information of the dungeon, from object space to world space. It does this so that we can actually figure out a) where our dungeons lie in the world, and b) whether other objects in the world intersect with them.

The latter is known as collision detection and is really important in game development.

Thankfully, we just need to add a BoxInfo property to our CellarDweller and we're all set!

# Instructions

Setting up our BoxInfo object is pretty easy. We just need to import it via require. I've been showing you how to do all of this require stuff, so why don't you give it a try? The BoxInfo object is found in the same utils file as the randomInt function we've already imported into our mod. Can you import it?

All right, now that you've done that, you'll have to construct a BoxInfo object in the constructor and set it as a property. You know where I'm going with this—do you think you can do it? You can call the property this.boxInfo, and the constructor requires location, width, and height as its arguments. If you have issues setting it up, take a look below for the answer.

```
// up in our require section
var BoxInfo = require('utils').BoxInfo;

// ... down in our CellarDweller Constructor
this.boxInfo = new BoxInfo(location, w, h);
```

# Random Entities: Part 6— Spawning, Nicely

 1    15–20 minutes

## Activity Overview

Did you notice some lag when you were spawning your enemies with FOR loops and while loops? When the server has to do a lot of hard work, it can hog the main process. The main process refers to the main processor thread that SpigotMC is running on. When we do things that are processor intensive, we can see that everything else lags around it.

Lucky for us, ScriptCraft has a function found in the utils module called nicely. What nicely does is actually schedule tasks that can be run asynchronously on the server. What does that mean? Well, it's a lot like the idea of event-driven programming we were talking about earlier. Normally, single-threaded, synchronous code runs one line after the other, just like how you write it. With asynchronous code, a function—or task—will be called, and then after some sort of delay, a provided callback will be called.

You already have some experience with asynchronous programming via events.on, so this shouldn't be too bad. What we're going to do is use utils.nicely to "nicely" add all our monsters to the world without hogging the main process. You're going to see some real speed increases!

## Instructions

Now we'll need a new method, and we'll also have to import the utils module:

```
// up at the top
var utils = require('utils');
```

```
// ... further down
CellarDweller.prototype.spawnRandomEntities = function() {
        // set up our tasks and run them!
}
```

The utils.nicely function works like this: it schedules a bunch of tasks to be run, one after the other. We provide functions that tell it whether or not there is another task (hasNext), what to do for with each task (next), what to do when all tasks are done (onDone), and the delay—in milliseconds—between each task. This is the order of the arguments:

1.  next: the actual task that is being run. In our case, this will be the function that spawns a single random monster at a single random location within the dungeon. We will also decrement (decrease by 1) a totalEntites count after we've spawned one, so that our hasNext function will work properly.
2.  hasNext: the function that determines whether or not we have any more tasks to be scheduled. This function has to return a Boolean for utils.nicely to work properly. We're going to check against a totalEntities variable that is decreased by 1 every time an entity is spawned. If totalEntities is 0, we return false and move on to onDone.
3.  onDone:the function that gets called once everything is done; usually, this is just some sort of status update, like "spawned *n* entities."
4.  Delay: the amount of time, in milliseconds, to wait between tasks. I'm setting this at 100ms, but you can try out different settings!

Now that we got that out of the way, let's start by setting up some preliminary variables, as well as our hasNext and onDone functions:

```
CellarDweller.prototype.spawnRandomEntities = function() {
    // random number of entities to spawn
  var totalEntities = this.getNumberOfEntities();
  /* the index to the current floor—we'll cycle through each floor
  to make sure everything gets dispersed properly */
  var currentFloor = 0;
  var hasNext = function() {
      return totalEntities > 0;
  }

  var onDone = function() {
      echo(self, "Successfully Spawned all entities!")
  }
}
```

Our hasNext just returns a Boolean value that evaluates whether or not our totalEntities are greater than 0. Every time we call our next function (which we'll write in the next activity), we'll subtract 1 from totalEntities so that hasNext will work properly. We're using the magic of closures again—both hasNext and next have access to that totalEntities variable because they were declared in the same scope—so we don't have to keep passing variables around.

# Random Entities: Part 7— In a Bind

 1   35–45 minutes

## Activity Overview

Now we should have everything in place to actually do our spawning. We're going to finish up our spawnRandomEntities method by writing the next function that gets passed to utils.nicely. To do that, I'm going to introduce you to my good friend the bind prototype method, which allows us to use our "this" variable within anonymous functions that we declare in our methods. Let's let some baddies loose in our dungeon!

# Instructions

We're about to discover one of JavaScript's unique little quirks firsthand. A lot of people have complained about this! I'm not complaining, myself, because there are easy ways to solve this issue. When we declare an anonymous function in one of our methods, we lose the reference to our "this" variable within the function scope. Let's use our next function as an example:

```
// hasNext and onDone functions are up here ^
var next = function() {
        echo(self, this.boxInfo);
}
next();
>> undefined
```

All that work we did just goes down the drain? Well, we could create closures by storing a reference to all the properties we need so that they're accessible within the next function:

```
// hasNext and onDone functions are up here ^
var boxInfo = this.boxInfo;
var next = function() {
        echo(self, boxInfo);
}
next();
>> [object Object]
```

This is known as the lexical scope, which sounds like some sort of alien medical instrument (and maybe it is—I can't say for sure, because I don't know any aliens). All you need to know about the lexical scope is that variables declared in the scope above our next function are accessible in that function—we just can't use "this."

It's kind of annoying having to create variables for every single property we need to access in our functions, isn't it? Well, thankfully the people behind the ECMAScript standard created a method called bind that we can use to bind, or replace the "this" context of our next function with whatever we choose. So if we pass our "this" variable to the bind method everything should work, right? Check out what that looks like:

```
// hasNext and onDone functions are up here ^
var next = function() {
        echo(self, this.boxInfo);
}.bind(this);
next();
>> [object Object]
```

Let's finish off the method. Remember, this is the task that gets scheduled every time hasNext returns true, so all we need to do is get a random monster, get a random point, and spawn the monster on one of our floors.

```
// hasNext and onDone functions are up here ^
var next = function() {
    var monster = this.getRandomMonster();
    var world = self.world;
    // BoxInfo.randomPoint needs a world in order to get a
    Location object
    var point = this.boxInfo.randomPoint(world);
    // spawn the monster
    spawn(monster, point);
        /* now we need to do some housekeeping—we'll cycle
    through our floors and decrement totalEntities */
```

```
    totalEntities -= 1; // could also do totalEntities--
    if (currentFloor === this.floors.length-1) {
            currentFloor = 0;
    } else {
            currentFloor += 1; // could also use currentFloor++
    }
}.bind(this);
```

The only thing that might be a little confusing here is what we're doing with the currentFloor variable. All we're doing is checking to see if we're at our top floor—if we are, we set the currentFloor index back to 0. That way, we're not spawning monsters on floors that don't exist, which would cause an error! Instead, we can cycle through our floors and evenly disperse the monsters.

Here is the spawnRandomEntities method in all its glory:

```
CellarDweller.prototype.spawnRandom = function() {
    var doSpawn = function(placeRandom, total) {
            var currentFloor = 0;
    var hasNext = function() {
            return total > 0;
    }

    var next = function() {
            var world = self.world;
            var point = this.boxInfo.randomPoint(world);
            // account for height of floors
            point.y = this.floors[currentFloor].location.y;
            placeRandom(point);
            total -= 1;
            if (currentFloor === this.floors.length-1) {
                currentFloor = 0;
            } else {
                currentFloor += 1;
            }
    }
```

```javascript
      }.bind(this);

    var onDone = function() {
      console.log("successfully spawned");
    }
      utils.nicely(next, hasNext, onDone, 100);
    }.bind(this);

  var totalItems = this.getNumberOfItems();
  var placeItem = function(point) {
      var item = this.getRandomItem();
      self.world.dropItem(point, item);
    }.bind(this);

  this.totalMonsters = this.getNumberOfEntities();
  var placeMonster = function(point) {
  var monster = this.getRandomMonster();
  spawn(monster, point);
  }.bind(this);

  // place all items
  doSpawn(placeItem, totalItems);
  // place all monsters
  doSpawn(placeMonster, this.totalMonsters);
}
```

# More Randomness: Part 1— Curated Items

 1  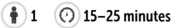 15–25 minutes

## Activity Overview

Now that we've got our handy BoxInfo.getRandomPoint method, we can just start dropping stuff everywhere! Because dungeon crawlers usually need more incentive beyond just battling monsters, we should be dropping some big-ticket items in there, too. In this activity, you're going to create a curated array of items to drop just like you did with the monsters.

## Instructions

All of the items available to you can be found here: https://hub .spigotmc.org/javadocs/bukkit/org/bukkit/Material.html.

Remember, the ScriptCraft items module works a bit differently from the entities one. For starters, the names are all camel cased rather than snake cased, and you can also pass in a parameter that specifies the amount of items in the ItemStack to be returned. Just like with CellarDweller.MONSTERS, I'll get you started. And oh yeah—don't forget to import the items module!

```
CellarDweller.LOOT = [
    items.chainmailHelmet(), // one helmet—could add more if
    you want
        // ... put the rest of your items down here
    ]
```

Don't skimp either! Put some really good stuff in there.

# More Randomness: Part 2—Picking an Item

 1  ⏱ 15–25 minutes

## Activity Overview

Now we have to come up with a getRandomItem method just like we did for getRandomMonster. As you start to work your way through the book and practice a bit more, it definitely helps to do a few things on your own without my help. It's one thing to be able to copy text and type it out—it's another thing to know what it's actually doing. So, here is my challenge to you: Can you write a getRandomItem method?

## Instructions

This one is all you! If you get stuck, use the getRandomMonster method as guidance. But try not to look at it if you can help it! All the method needs to do is return a random item from our CellarDweller.LOOT array. You can do it!

I wasn't joking about copying text! It's really important, especially when you first start out programming, that you get some practice doing independent problem solving without looking at every step of the code. The best way to learn is by doing! And how did it go? It wasn't that bad, was it? Just double-check that your answer looks like this:

```javascript
CellarDweller.prototype.getRandomItem = function() {
  var loot = CellarDweller.LOOT;
  var index = randomInt(0, loot.length - 1);
  return loot[index];
}
```

# More Randomness: Part 3—A Little Snag

 1    15–25 minutes

## Activity Overview

I just noticed something. If we want to have the amount of loot in the dungeon based on a difficulty level, shouldn't the difficulty level be inverted? If the difficulty is set to "easy," the players should get more loot, not less.

Well, this is something we all have to do eventually. You have to adapt your code for other features that you add as you go on. You can't account for everything, although you can certainly try. In the cases where you don't, you'll have to write some more code to piece together the new features. Here we go again with some more of that "creative problem solving" I keep talking about.

## Instructions

We can use our existing CellarDweller.DIFFICULTY object and invert the difficulty values. We need to make sure that we don't modify our CellarDweller.DIFFICULTY object in place, meaning we don't modify the original object. Instead, we need to create a new object so we don't have any unexpected behavior. Only twenty-five monsters on "insane" difficulty? That's too easy! We could just create another object by hand, but where's the fun in that?

Let's create a function called invertDifficulty, which will take a property (key), invert our difficulty levels, and return the new value for that key. This doesn't need to be part of CellarDweller, but just an internal, or private, function. Because we're not exporting it, and it's not part of CellarDweller, the only way we can call it is in our index.js file.

```
function invertDifficulty(level) {
    // let's also create an array to store our values in
    var values = [];
    var keys = [];
    // remember for ... in? We use that to push all of the values
    onto the values array
    for (var key in CellarDweller.DIFFICULTY) {
        keys.push(key);
        values.push(CellarDweller.DIFFICULTY[key];
    }
    // now what we can do is reverse the array
    values.reverse();
        // our inverted object
    var inverted = {};
        // iterate over all of the keys
    keys.forEach(function(key, index) {
        inverted[key] = values[index];
    });
    return inverted[level];
}
```

Okay, this probably needs some explanation. We're going to create two empty arrays, one to store our keys and one to store our values. By using for ... in, we can populate the arrays. We then use the reverse method to invert the elements in the values array. So far, so good. Finally, we create a new empty object called inverted, and set the keys and values by iterating over the keys array with forEach. Finally, we return the new, inverted value based on the level. That's it!

# More Randomness: Part 4—How Many Items Can We Drop?

 1  15–25 minutes

## Activity Overview

Unlike with entities, SpigotMC has no limit on the number of items you can drop in your world. But we still need a way to come up with a decent amount of items to randomly disperse—not too many, not too few. What do you think? Maybe we base it off of the size of our dungeon layout. You're more than welcome to come up with your own metrics for determining how many items to drop based on difficulty—in fact, I encourage it! For now, though, try my way.

## Instructions

You guessed it: we're going to create a method called getNumberOfItems just like we did with getNumberOfEntities. This one will be quite different, though, because we don't need to follow the limit of around seventy items that we did with monsters. We probably shouldn't base our number off of the total area of our dungeon because that'll result in way too many items. What if we base it off of the longest side of our layout?

We could do something like this:

- Find the longest side of the layout (compare this.w to this.h).
- Obtain our max value by multiplying the longest side by this.itemDifficulty.
- Obtain our min value by dividing our max in half.
- Use randomInt to return a value between min and max.

By the way, I think you've reached a point where you can build this method based on the previous steps. If you run into trouble, take a look at getNumberOfEntities. Also, you can look below to see my answer—but try it on your own first!

```
CellarDweller.prototype.getNumberOfItems = function() {
    var longest = this.w > this.h ? this.w : this.h;
    var max = Math.floor(longest * this.itemDifficulty);
    var min = max / 2;
    return randomInt(min, max);
}
```

# More Randomness: Part 5— Refactoring

 1   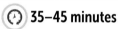 35–45 minutes

## Activity Overview

Now we have a bunch of methods for getting random items and monsters. We still need to write a method that randomly drops all of our items in our dungeon. Or do we? Because the actual execution of dropping items and spawning monsters is quite similar, we're actually going to refactor—or rewrite—a portion of our spawnRandomEntities method so that it can handle both monsters and items.

## Instructions

We'll start by changing the name of our spawnRandomEntities method to something more appropriate—why don't we call it spawnRandom? Let's figure out what our current method does that's unique to spawning monsters:

1.  It calls getRandomMonster to, well, get a random monster.
2.  It calls getTotalNumberOfEntites to get the total entities.
3.  It uses the spawn function to spawn the monster.

Well, I think we may have found three parameters for our new function. Here's the more generic version of the above:

1.  A function to randomly provide any sort of item or entity.
2.  A count for the total number of things to drop or spawn.
3.  A function to do the spawning.

We have what we need, and we can even make it simpler by combining our random item and monster generation code with the placement (spawning, dropping) code. Now we're down to two params!

Let's start by wrapping all of our utils.nicely code in a new function called doSpawn:

```
CellarDweller.prototype.spawnRandomEntities = function() {
  var doSpawn = function(placeRandom, total) {}

}
```

doSpawn will take a placeRandom function, which takes a location provided by doSpawn, as well as a total number of items and monsters to spawn. Let's write those functions, which will live below doSpawn.

```
// ... doSpawn up here ^

var totalItems = this.getNumberOfItems();
var placeItem = function(point) {
```

```javascript
    var item = this.getRandomItem();
    self.world.dropItem(point, item);
}.bind(this);

var totalMonsters = this.getNumberOfEntities();
var placeMonster = function(point) {
    var monster = this.getRandomMonster();
    spawn(monster, point);
}.bind(this);
```

Look familiar, don't they? Pretty simple, they just take a point and place their random item or monster there. The totalItems and totalMonsters variables should be pretty self-explanatory by now.

Now we just need to clean up our next function, which is now within doSpawn:

```javascript
var next = function() {
    var world = self.world;
    var point = this.boxInfo.randomPoint(world);
    // account for height of floors
    point.y = this.floors[currentFloor].location.y;
    placeRandom(point);
    total -= 1;
    if (currentFloor === this.floors.length-1) {
    currentFloor = 0;
    } else {
    currentFloor += 1;
    }
}.bind(this);
```

We still calculate the point variable in our next function because we need access to currentFloor. Other than that, we've cleaned everything up—now placeRandom replaces all of the other steps for spawning or dropping in the next function. Not bad!

Finally, we just need to call doSpawn with the proper params:

```javascript
// place all items
doSpawn(placeItem, totalItems);
// place all monsters
doSpawn(placeMonster, totalMonsters);
```

And finally, the code in all its glory:

```javascript
CellarDweller.prototype.spawnRandomEntities = function() {
    var doSpawn = function(placeRandom, total) {
      var currentFloor = 0;
      var hasNext = function() {
          return total > 0;
      }

      var next = function() {
        var world = self.world;
        var point = this.boxInfo.randomPoint(world);
        // account for height of floors
        point.y = this.floors[currentFloor].location.y;
        placeRandom(point);
        total -= 1;
        if (currentFloor === this.floors.length-1) {
          currentFloor = 0;
        } else {
          currentFloor += 1;
        }
      }.bind(this);

      var onDone = function() {
       console.log("successfully spawned");
      }

      utils.nicely(next, hasNext, onDone, 100);
```

```
    }.bind(this);

    var totalItems = this.getNumberOfItems();
    var placeItem = function(point) {
    var item = this.getRandomItem();
    self.world.dropItem(point, item);
    }.bind(this);

    var totalMonsters = this.getNumberOfEntities();
    var placeMonster = function(point) {
    var monster = this.getRandomMonster();
    spawn(monster, point);
    }.bind(this);

    // place all items
    doSpawn(placeItem, totalItems);
    // place all monsters
    doSpawn(placeMonster, totalMonsters);
}
```

# Document, Document, Document!

I know what you're thinking. "Documentation? I want to learn about programming, not documentation!" But trust me: Documentation doesn't need to be a long, boring process. We can use something called JSDoc, which has become one of the most popular document generation tools available for JavaScript. Although not totally automatic, it takes a lot of pain out of the process, allows you to do your documentation right in your source files, and produces some really nice static web pages you can serve up for other developers to read.

# Finding Order in Chaos

 1    25–30 minutes

## Activity Overview

Documentation is essential to any software project, and up to this point we haven't really done any. We're going to try to go back to our Cellar Dweller code and group similar methods together, as well as provide documentation via something called JSDoc, which can be used to automatically generate a webpage documenting our CellarDweller program—pretty cool! JSDoc works a lot like Javadoc, which was used to make all of the SpigotMC documentation we've been looking at. In my opinion, using a tool like this will help you build your documentation as you go along and helps keep it up to date because it lives right in your source code files.

## Instructions

Let's start by organizing our methods a bit. I like to group similar methods by what they do. Take a few minutes and read through all of our Cellar Dweller code and see if you can group similar methods together in the file as best as you can.

Now that you've done that, we can take a look at the JSDoc syntax. When you run your source file through a JSDoc generator, it looks for comments that have special characters in them, called tags. These tags allow us to provide more information about our code, and they also allow the JSDoc generator to lay out the information in a clear and appealing way. It's pretty easy to get the hang of! We want to document the following:

- A description of our object, method, or function
- Its parameters, if any
- Its return value, if any

Let's start by describing our CellarDweller constructor:

```
/**
 * Constructs a CellarDweller instance
 * @constructor
 * @param {org.bukkit.Location} location—The location to build
   the dungeon.
 * @param {number} width—The width of the dungeon layout
 * @param {number} height—The height of the dungeon layout
 * @param {object} options—Optional parameters
 * @param {number} options.nFloors—The number of floors in
   the dungeon
 * @param {number} options.depth—The depth (height) of
   each floor
 * @param {string} options.difficulty—The difficulty level—options
   are 'easy', 'medium', 'difficult', and 'insane'
 * @param {number} options.iterations—The number of iterations
   for generating the BSP layout—default is 4
 * @param {org.bukkit.Material} options.blockType—The type of
   block to use to build the dungeon—default is stone
 * @param {DungeonMaker.DOORTYPE} options.doorType—The
   type of door to use on the dungeons. Options are 'door',
   'door2', 'iron', 'door2_iron', and 'random'—default is 'random'
 * @param {DungeonMaker.LIGHTMODE} options.lightMode—
   The type of lighting—options are 'dark', 'dim', 'medium', and
   'bright'—default is 'medium'
*/
var CellarDweller = function(location, w, h, options) {
// ... rest of the CellarDweller code is down here
```

That one looks pretty complicated, but it's the hardest one we have to do because of all of the options passed down to Drone-Dungeon. Check out the next one, which is much easier:

```
/**
 * CellarDweller difficulty options
 * @readonly
 * @enum {number}
```

```
*/
CellarDweller.DIFFICULTY = {
    easy: 0.25, // 1/8 of the max value
    medium: 0.5, // 1/2 of the max value
    difficult: 0.75, // 3/4 of the max value
    insane: 1 // the max value
}
```

And properties ...

```
/**
* CellarDweller monster array
* @readonly
* @static
*/
CellarDweller.MONSTERS = [
    // ... monsters here
];
```

Finally, a method that returns something:

```
/**
* Returns a random number of monsters based on world.
getMonsterSpawnLimit
* @return {number}
*/
CellarDweller.prototype.getNumberOfEntities = function() {
    var world = self.world;
    var max = world.getMonsterSpawnLimit() * this.difficulty;
    var min = max / 2;
    return randomInt(min, max);
}
```

You should have all of the info you need to go through and document the rest of the rest of the methods and properties we have. Give it a go!

# Checking Our Work Again

 1  ⏱ 20–30 minutes

## Activity Overview

Now we're actually going to try running JSDoc on our CellarDweller module so we can see if our documentation worked. We'll have to install NodeJS (you probably want this on your computer anyway) and then install and run JSDoc.

## Instructions

### Installing NodeJS on Windows

1. Download the latest NodeJS LTS (long-term support) installer from https://nodejs.org/en/download.
2. Once the installer has downloaded, run it and follow the installation instructions.
3. Restart your machine.

### Installing NodeJS on a Mac

1. Download the latest NodeJS LTS (long-term support) OSX installer from https://nodejs.org/en/download.
2. Double-click on the .pkg file and follow the installation instructions.

To test to see if NodeJS works, open up a terminal or command prompt and type: node We're going to use npm, the Node Package Manager, to install JSDoc—npm pulls modules from repositories and installs them for you and is a gateway to a huge library of JavaScript modules.

Important note: You cannot run NodeJS code with ScriptCraft. NodeJS and Nashorn are two completely different JavaScript engines.

To install JSDoc globally, all we have to do is type: npm install -g jsdoc.

The "-g" flag installs the jsdoc tool globally, so it can be run from the command prompt like this: jsdoc myfile.js (or mydirectory).

All we need to do now is change directories to {your -spigotmc-directory}/scriptcraft/modules/cellar-dweller (on Windows it would be {your-spigotmc-directory}\scriptcraft \modules\cellar-dweller). Now you can run: jsdoc index.js. You should see a new folder called Out. If you open up that folder, you can double-click on the index.html file or drag it and drop it into your web browser and you should see a homepage:

# Home

Home

Classes

CellarDweller

Now click on CellarDweller and you should see

# Class: CellarDweller

Home

Classes

CellarDweller

## CellarDweller(location, width, height, options)

new CellarDweller(location, width, height, options)

Constructs a CellarDweller instance

**Parameters:**

| Name | Type | Description | | | |
|------|------|-------------|--|--|--|
| location | org.bukkit.Location | The location to build the dungeon. | | | |
| width | number | The width of the dungeon layout | | | |
| height | number | The height of the dungeon layout | | | |
| options | Object | Optional parameters | | | |
| | | *Properties* | | | |
| | | Name | Type | Description | |
| | | nFloors | number | The number of floors in the dungeon | |
| | | depth | number | The depth (height) of each floor | |
| | | difficulty | string | The difficulty level - options are 'easy', 'medium', 'difficult', and 'insane' | |

## Functional Programming

Functional programming is another key paradigm supported by JavaScript. It takes a bit of getting used to, but it makes for some really concise code. In particular, we'll try out some declarative methods like map, filter, and reduce, which perform operations on arrays in really interesting ways!

# I Do Declare: Part 1— Array Map

 1   ⏱ 20–30 minutes

## Activity Overview

Now that you've got parts of your Cellar Dweller mod up and running, your mission is to clean up your code and do some functional programming. In a basic sense, functional programming treats functions as higher-order objects, immutable data structures, and declarative syntax. That's a lot of vocabulary!

First, what are higher-order functions? It's just a fancy way of saying that we can pass around functions just like we can with any other data type. We can store them as object properties, we can use them as arguments to other functions, and we can return them from functions. It may not sound exciting yet, but stay with me.

Immutable data is also a pretty simple concept with an impressive name. It just means that our functions should not modify state in place, but they should make a copy of the state we're interested in, and then modify that.

And what about declarative programming? Well, you spent a lot of time dealing with control flow in some earlier activities, and your mod currently has a lot of it. Declarative programming is a paradigm that is more concerned with what a block of code or function does, rather than how it's implemented. The name of the paradigm is actually pretty clear: you're *declaring* what you want a function to do!

The opposite of this is called imperative programming, which is more procedural in nature—for instance, you're describing how your program iterates over arrays with FOR and while loops.

# Instructions

A lot of functional languages take advantage of a declarative paradigm. The map function takes a function as an argument, applies it to every element in an array, and returns an array containing modified copies of those elements. Let's put it this way: your mod code would be a lot more cluttered without a map function!

In our Cellar Dweller mod, we have our array, which holds information about our generated floors stored as a property called this.floors. Because you may want to expose information about our dungeon to another program—but want to make that information read only—you can use map to return a copy of the array that shows only the stuff you want to expose. Start off by creating a new method called getFloors.

Your JSDoc documentation should look like this:

```
/**
* Get an array of objects with information about each floor
* @return {Array} the array of floors
*/
```

Now, our method declaration:

```
CellarDweller.prototype.getFloors = function() {

}
```

Remember, Array.prototype.map returns an array, so we can have our method actually return the Array.prototype.map method.

```
CellarDweller.prototype.getFloors = function() {
    return this.floors.map();
}
```

As cool as that method looks, it doesn't do anything yet—it returns undefined. Remember, Array.prototype.map is a higher-order function, so it takes a function as a parameter—just like the Array.forEach method we've used. The only difference is that our prior use of Array.forEach introduced side effects into our code.

Side effects are created when you modify state that exists outside of the scope of your method or function. This is pretty much unavoidable in object-oriented programming and isn't necessarily a bad thing. Array.forEach returns undefined because it's designed to be a more declarative version of a FOR loop.

This is how we pass an anonymous function as an argument to Array.prototype.map:

```
CellarDweller.prototype.getFloors = function() {
    return this.floors.map(function(floor) {
        // deal with floor here
    });
}
```

Within that function body, we can create a new object with all of the floor properties we want to expose and return that:

```
CellarDweller.prototype.getFloors = function() {
```

```
    // maybe we just want to provide the location and
    the rooms?
    return this.floors.map(function(floor) {
        var floorInfo = {};
        // maybe other devs want to keep track of the rooms
        floorInfo.rooms = floor.rooms;
        // or maybe they want to get the location to, say,
        create a custom map
        floorInfo.location = floor.location;
        return floorInfo;
    });
}
```

Now you have a method that returns a read-only copy of the info you want about your dungeons! In the next few activities, you're going to look at how you can filter a subset of our rooms, or how to flatten everything into a 2D array.

# I Do Declare: Part 2—Flattener

 1  20–30 minutes

## Activity Overview

That map method is pretty handy. Sometimes, you may want to return a flat array instead of a multi-dimensional one—for instance, if we just want a flat array of all rooms, rather than rooms separated by floors. We'll create a method called getRooms and use Array .prototype.reduce to take all of the rooms from and "reduce" them down to a single array.

## Instructions

Before we can start, let's make sure we add some JSDoc info to this one too:

```
/**
 * Get a flat array of objects with information about each room in
the dungeon
 * @return {Array} the array of rooms
 */
CellarDweller.prototype.getRooms = function() {
        // do some flattening!
}
```

The way Array.prototype.reduce works is kind of like map or forEach. It also applies a callback function to every element of an array. The difference, however, is that the first parameter passed to the callback is an accumulator. The accumulator accumulates each value that gets returned by the callback. The second parameter passed to the callback is the current value in the array. The easiest way to explain this is with an example:

```
var summed = [1, 2, 3, 4].reduce(function(accumulator, currentValue) {
        // we keep adding currentValue to the accumulator at
        each iteration
        return accumulator + currentValue;
});
echo(self, summed);
>> 10
```

The result is 10 because 1 + 2 + 3 + 4 = 10. Is that cool or what? So what about accumulating arrays? We can actually use the Array.prototype.concat to concatenate (combine or merge) the arrays, just like we can with strings:

```
CellarDweller.prototype.getRooms = function() {
    return this.floors.reduce(function(accumulator, floor) {
            return accumulator.concat(floor.rooms);
    }, []);
}
```

This method starts with an empty array (the second parameter passed to reduce after the callback) and keeps merging each floor's rooms arrays with the accumulator. What we end up with is a single flat array of rooms.

The only problem with this method is that we don't know which floor the rooms are on! Well, maybe we don't care. But let's say we do. Luckily, there's a third param passed to the callback: currentIndex, which is the currentIndex in our floors array that corresponds to the current value. In other words, our floor index. Now we can do some crazy Jedi stuff:

```
CellarDweller.prototype.getRooms = function() {
    return this.floors.reduce(function(accumulator, floor, currentIndex) {
        var modifiedRooms = floor.rooms.map(function
        (room) {
            room.floorIndex = currentIndex;
            return room;
        });
        return accumulator.concat(modifiedRooms);
    }, []);
}
```

See what we did there? We used a map on each floor's rooms property to return a copy of each room with a new property called floorIndex. We then merge all of the rooms into one flat array like before!

# I Do Declare: Part 3—Filter

 1   20–30 minutes

## Activity Overview

The last in the trinity of functional programming array operations, filter iterates over an array and applies a callback to every element and returns a Boolean, not the element itself. Why? We're telling the filter method what to keep and what to leave out of the resulting array. We'll add a method that allows the user to provide their own filtering criteria for our rooms data. It's not particularly useful right now, but hey, if you learn something, then it's going to be useful eventually!

## Instructions

Just like we did with Array.prototype.reduce, let's look at a generic example of how filter works:

```
var greaterThan3 = [1, 2, 3, 4, 5, 6].filter(function(element) {
        return element > 3;
});
echo(self, greaterThan3);
>> [4, 5, 6]
```

What filter does is copy the elements that meet the criteria (in this case, numbers that are larger than 3) out of our source array and put them in a new array.

We can write a filterRooms method that takes a callback as a parameter. The JSDoc looks a little bit different for callbacks—check it out:

```
/**
* Filter all of the rooms in the dungeon based on a callback function
* @param {CellarDweller~filterCallback} callback—The callback that
determines what rooms to filter.
*/
CellarDweller.prototype.filterRooms = function(callback) {
  return this.getRooms().filter(callback);
}
```

What is CellarDweller~filterCallback? With JSDoc, we can also supply documentation for callbacks, specifically the parameters that they take as well as their return value. Below my filterRooms method, I provide that additional info:

```
/**
* This callback determines which rooms to filter with the
filterRooms method
* @callback CellarDweller~filterCallback
* @param {Object} room—A room from the dungeon
* @returns {boolean}—Whether or not the room should be filtered
*/
```

So all that CellarDweller~filterCallback does is provide a connection between the callback and the method that uses it as a parameter. I know it's kind of confusing, but look at how clear it makes everything when the documentation is generated. Here is the method definition:

**filterRooms(callback)**

Filter all of the rooms in the dungeon based on a callback function

**Parameters:**

| Name | Type | Description |
|------|------|-------------|
| callback | CellarDweller~filterCallback | The callback that determines what rooms to filter. |

Source:  index.js, line 137

And the callback—which is linked under the type field:

```
filterCallback(room) → {boolean}
```

This callback determines which rooms to filter with the filterRooms method

**Parameters:**

| Name | Type | Description |
|------|------|-------------|
| room | Object | A room from the dungeon |

Source: index.js, line 141

**Returns:**

- Whether or not the room should be filtered

Type

   boolean

See the method? All it does is call this.getRooms and then chains that map with a filter:

return this.getRooms().filter(callback);

Super simple and clean! Now people can use it like this. Let's pretend we have a CellarDweller instance called cd, and we want to get all of the rooms that are smaller than a given area. Now we can do that!

```
var area = 80;
var smallRooms = cd.filterRooms(function(room) {
    return room.w * room.h < area;
});
```

That's it, folks! It all comes together.

## Getting Interactive with Events

We've done a little bit of event-driven programming up to this point, but now we'll get right into it. We'll install a module called event dispatcher, which will let us listen to and dispatch events so we can start to add some custom interactivity to our mod!

# The Big Event: Part 1—Set-Up

 1     15–20 minutes

## Activity Overview

The end is in sight! Now we've got to set up our event system, which can attach handlers to all SpigotMC events. It'll also be able to dispatch its own events, which other plugins can listen to via the custom ScriptCraftEvent class. We're going to import the event-dispatcher module, and set up an initEvents method that we can call in our constructor to attach all of our handlers to the specific events we want to listen to. Although it's pretty morbid, we're going to be listening to the entityDeath method for every time an entity is killed (RIP) and check if it happens in our dungeon. Similarly, we'll be listening to the playerPickupItem event to check if players are picking up items in our dungeon.

## Instructions

We'll have to go ahead and download the event-dispatcher module from https://github.com/jjromphf/scriptcraft-cellar-dweller-mod. Installing this is going to be a little different than what we're used to. I wrote the event-dispatcher module to listen to and dispatch events within ScriptCraft and Nashorn, with the option of listening to native Java events, and dispatching a custom ScriptCraftEvent that allows other SpigotMC Java plugins to listen and react to what's going on in our mod.

Thankfully, that stuff is all done behind the scenes. Because of this piece of the puzzle, we'll have to install both the JS files and a Java .jar file. The downloading and unzipping instructions are the same as those you followed in The Mod Squad activity.

Now there's one more step. Inside that event-dispatcher folder is a file called event-dispatcher.jar. This is just like the ScriptCraft .jar file we installed at the beginning of chapter two—it's packaged Java code that goes into the plugins directory of your SpigotMC folder. So, if you want to support native events, you can copy that event-dispatcher.jar file to {your-spigotmc-dir}/plugins and restart the server. We should be good to go!

Now, we need to create three methods: one called initEvents, which registers all of our event handlers, one called handleEntityDeath, which will be called for every events .entityDeath event, and one called handlePlayerPickupItem, which will be called for every events.playerPickupItem event. First, we require the event-dispatcher module:

```
// other require files are up here
var EventDispatcher = require('event-dispatcher');
/**
* Initializes all internal event handlers for CellarDweller
*/
CellarDweller.prototype.initEvents = function() {
    EventDispatcher.on('entityDeath', this.handleEntityDeath.
bind(this);
    EventDispatcher.on('playerPickupItem', this.
handlePlayerPickupItem.bind(this);
}
```

EventDispatcher is what we call a singleton object—it's an object that can only be instantiated once. That way, when it's imported into other files, all of the event listeners and dispatches are done at a global level. Our handlers are handled (ha!) like so:

```
/**
 * Event handler for org.bukkit.event.entity.EntityDeathEvent
 * @param {Object} event—the EntityDeathEvent
 */
CellarDweller.prototype.handleEntityDeath = function(event) {
        // handle the event
}
```

The last step is to call this.initEvents in your constructor—can you do it? Well, I hope so because that's the activity!

# The Big Event: Part 2— Monster Slayer

 1     15–20 minutes

## Activity Overview

Now that we have the skeletons of our handlers set up, we're going to start with our handleEntityDeath handler. We need to check for a few things:

- The location of where the event took place so we can figure out if it was in our dungeon.
- If it was, get information about the player who did it, as well as the type of monster.
- Keep track of that player and their stats within the dungeon
- Update how many monsters are in our dungeon.

This will require a bit of refactoring across the next few activities, but it shouldn't be too bad. We're going to be tackling more state in our program, which is data that stays in memory and is updated or changed.

# Instructions

Remember when we used our getNumberOfEntities method to get a random number of monsters in our dungeon based on difficulty? We forgot to add a way to keep track of that! We need to store it in a property so we can keep updating it every time someone whacks a monster in our dungeon. We just start by stating our intentions in our constructor:

**//put this somewhere in your CellarDweller constructor**
**this**.totalMonsters = null;

Now, down in our spawnRandomEntitiesMethod, we can do a little rearranging. We'll change this:

**var** totalMonsters = **this**.getNumberOfEntities();

To this:

**this**.totalMonsters = **this**.getNumberOfEntities();
**// further down**
doSpawn(placeMonster, **this**.totalMonsters);

I know what you're thinking: "but don't we decrement that number when we pass it to our doSpawn function? Doesn't that mean this.totalMonsters will be 0 once we've spawned them all?" Well, that's a really good question! Some languages, like C and C++, support something called pass by reference. What that means is you can actually pass a reference to a variable to a function (actually, a memory address), so you can operate on the original variable. This is useful if you need to save memory or increase performance, but not really ideal for what we're doing. A lot of other languages use something called pass by value, meaning that variables passed to a function or method are copied to the local scope of the function. This is a very long-winded way of me saying that our this.totalMonsters property will be safe even though we're passing it to doSpawn and it's being operated on.

Okay, let's write our handleEntityDeath method. JSDoc has some cool features for documenting events. Let's take a look! Just like what were doing with documenting callbacks, we can actually reference a specific event via the @listens tag. We could also define the event in our file, but because it's a native Java event, that's kind of pointless. So we'll just do this:

```
/**
 * Event handler for org.bukkit.event.entity.EntityDeathEvent
 * @listens org.bukkit.event.entity~EntityDeathEvent
 * @param {Object} event—the EntityDeathEvent
 */
CellarDweller.prototype.handleEntityDeath = function(event) { ...
```

If I go ahead and run jsdoc, I get this:

## handleEntityDeath(event)

Event handler for org.bukkit.event.entity.EntityDeathEvent

### Parameters:

| Name | Type | Description |
| --- | --- | --- |
| event | Object | the EntityDeathEvent |

| Source: | index.js, line 256 |
| --- | --- |

### Listens to Events:

- org.bukkit.event~event:EntityDeathEvent

Not bad! But not that descriptive. I guess we could put in a link to the SpigotMC documentation in the description. The @link tag works like this: You put the url of the link first, followed by a space, followed by the text representing the link, which will be highlighted and clickable:

```
/**
* Event handler for {@link https://hub.spigotmc.org/javadocs/
spigot/org/bukkit/event/entity/EntityDeathEvent.html org.bukkit.
event.entity.EntityDeathEvent}
* @listens org.bukkit.event.entity~EntityDeathEvent
* @param {Object} event—the EntityDeathEvent
*/
CellarDweller.prototype.handleEntityDeath = function(event) { ...
```

And that gets us some nice hyperlinked text that goes out to the SpigotMC docs.

We've finally reached the method part. The event should have a couple of useful properties—entity, which is the entity that died, and location, which is the location.

```
CellarDweller.prototype.handleEntityDeath = function(event) {
    // figure out if it's a monster
    var entity = event.entity;
    if (entity instanceof Java.type("org.bukkit.entity.Monster")) {
        if (this.boxInfo.containsPoint(entity.location)) {
        this.totalMonsters -= 1;
        }
    }
}
```

Not overly complicated. All we have to do is check to see if the entity is a monster. For that, we can use the Java statement instanceof, which returns a Boolean if the entity is either an instance of, or inherits from, the given class (which is supplied as the right operand).

After that, all we have to do is check to see if our boxInfo

object contains our location. We can use the boxInfo
.containsPoint method, which takes an org.bukkit.Location as its
only argument. This is another example of collision detection.
The method returns true if the location falls within the inside
of our boxInfo object, which contains information about the
position, width, and height of our dungeon.

Now that we know that a player has slayed a monster in
our dungeon, we can go ahead and scratch one off the list by
decrementing our totalMonsters property by 1. We're interactive now!

# The Big Event: Part 3— Scavenger Hunt

 1   15–20 minutes

## Activity Overview

Now that we've successfully checked for monster slayings in our
dungeon, we can also handle all of the org.bukkit.event.player
.PlayerPickupItem events. We'll follow the exact same pattern as
before. And, actually, this one is a little easier. Maybe we want to try
to echo the player and the item that was picked up in order to make
things a little more interesting!

## Instructions

Let's add some more of that JSDoc goodness to our handler method.

```
/**
* Event handler for {@link Can you find the URL in the docs? org.
bukkit.event.player.PlayerPickupItemEvent}
* @listens org.bukkit.event.player~PlayerPickupItemEvent
* @param {Object} event—the PlayerPickupItemEvent
*/
```

```
CellarDweller.prototype.handlePlayerPickupItem = function(event) {
    // what do we do?
}
```

I purposefully left the link blank so that you could try to find it. (Hint: The package name is very similar to the URL.)

Once you've found that link, we can go ahead and take care of business. There are three properties set on this event that are of interest to us: the player that picked up the item, the location of that player, and the type of item they picked up. If the location checks out, we can decrement out totalItems property by 1.

```
CellarDweller.prototype.handlePlayerPickupItem = function(event) {
    var player = event.player;
    if (this.boxInfo.containsPoint(player.location)) {
        this.totalItems -= 1;
        echo(self, player.name + " picked up a " + event.item.
        name);
    }
}
```

All we have to do is check the player's location, just like before. If that checks out, we're home free to do whatever we want!

# The Big Event: Part 4: Dispatcher

 1     15–20 minutes

## Activity Overview

Now that we have our two handlers set up, we can actually dispatch some additional information in some events of our own. Yes, we can create our own events with EventDispatcher—we're running this show now!

## Instructions

We'll start with our handleEntityDeath method. Let's say we want to come up with some sort of "monster death" event that's specific to CellarDweller. EventDispatcher makes it really easy to dispatch events. There's a dispatch method that takes two parameters: the first is the name of the event you want to dispatch, and the second is an object that contains information you want to send along with the event. Because we're actually coming up with our events, we can declare them in our index.js file and document them via JSDoc.

Our events are going to be super simple—we can put them down at the bottom of our index.js file if we want:

```
// events
/**
* Monster Slay event
* @event CellarDweller#MonsterSlay
* @type {object}
* @property {string} monster—the type of monster
* @property {org.bukkit.Entity} entity—the entity info for
```

```
the monster
* @property {org.bukkit.Location} location—the location of
the slaying
* @property {org.bukkit.entity.Player} player—the player that did
the slaying
*/
CellarDweller.MonsterSlay = 'MonsterSlay';
```

We're just documenting the properties that we're going to send via our dispatched object. Our CellarDweller.MonsterSlay is just a string—the name of the event we pass as the first parameter to the dispatch static method.

Now let's update our handleEntityDeath method to dispatch an event:

```
/**
* Event handler for {@link https://hub.spigotmc.org/javadocs/
spigot/org/bukkit/event/entity/EntityDeathEvent.html org.bukkit.
event.entity.EntityDeathEvent}
* @listens org.bukkit.event~EntityDeathEvent
* @param {Object} event—the EntityDeathEvent
* @fires CellarDweller#MonsterSlay
*/
CellarDweller.prototype.handleEntityDeath = function(event) {
  // figure out if it's a monster
  var entity = event.entity;
  if (entity instanceof Java.type("org.bukkit.entity.Monster")) {
  if (this.boxInfo.containsPoint(entity.location)) {
    this.totalMonsters -= 1;
    // start of updated code
    var info = {
     entity: entity,
     location: location,
     player: entity.getKiller(),
     monster: entity.name,
```

```
    }
    EventDispatcher.dispatch(CellarDweller.MonsterSlayEvent,
        info);
    // end of updated code


        }
    }
}
```

All we have to do is create an object with all of the additional info we want to dispatch. Everything is pretty standard, except for the entity.getKiller method, which returns whatever entity killed the dead entity. In our case, it should be a player—so we'll call it player. Now, the dispatch static method is pretty straightforward, we have CellarDweller.MonsterSlayEvent as the event name, and our info object as the object.

With that, other ScriptCraft developers can use EventDispatcher.on(CellarDweller.MonsterSlayEvent, callback) to attach listeners to our event. SpigotMC developers can also listen via the native ScriptCraft event whose eventType property will be MonsterSlayEvent. This thing is really coming together! Give it a try and import EventDispatcher into ScriptCraft and see if you can listen to our events.

# The Big Event: Part 5: DIY (Dispatch It Yourself)

 1    ⏱ 15–20 minutes

## Activity Overview

You pretty much have all of the pieces of this puzzle now. All we need to do is add an ItemPickedUp event to our CellarDweller module so we can dispatch some info whenever a player picks up an item in our dungeon. I'm going to go ahead and provide you with the JSDoc info for the event, and then it's up to you to DIY— dispatch it yourself. All you have to do is follow the same pattern established in our handleEntityDeath and pass an info object with the correct properties as the second argument of the dispatch method!

## Instructions

This is the event description for our ItemPickedUp event, along with the static property definition:

```
// MonsterSlay event up here ^
/**
* ItemPickedUp event
* @event CellarDweller#ItemPickedUp
* @type {object}
* @property {string} item—the type of item
* @property {org.bukkit.Location} location—the location where the
item was picked up
* @property {org.bukkit.entity.Player} player—the player that picked
up the item
*/
CellarDweller.ItemPickedUp = 'ItemPickedUp';
```

## Persistence

We're on the final stretch! We'll talk about serialization and persistence (saving our state) and will come up with a couple of static methods that will allow us to save all of the data about our CellarDweller instances and load them back into *Minecraft* after the server has shut down.

# Being Persistent: Part 1— Player State

 1    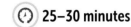 25–30 minutes

## Activity Overview

To make this even more interactive, we can add a bit more state to our CellarDweller mod. We can keep track of all of the players on the server who have either slayed a monster or picked up an item in our dungeon. All we have to do is come up with a data structure, which can then be saved before the server is shut down and loaded every time the server starts up. First, we'll decide on what we want to track and we'll come up with a property for it—then we'll write a method that we can call to update it whenever a player picks up an item or slays a monster!

## Instructions

For now, here's the information that we'd like to keep track of:

- The player
- How many monsters they've slayed
- How many items they've picked up

Rather than an array of players, we can actually use the player's universally unique identifier (UUID), which is a unique id that we can reference all of our players by in order to not overwrite their data. Thankfully, SpigotMC already generates a UUID for every entity, so our job is pretty easy! In our constructor, let's initialize a property called playerData:

```
this.playerData = {};
```

Now we can make a method to update our player data. It's pretty important that we do all of our updating via this method, rather than updating the state all over the place. Unfortunately, unlike Java, we can't set any explicitly private properties, but at least if we write an updatePlayerData method, we can express our intention: that we want other developers to use that method rather setting the properties elsewhere. Let's start with this:

```
/**
 * Updates a CellarDweller instance's playerData
 * @param {string} uuid—the player's uuid
 * @param {object} data—the player data we want to update
 * @param {number} data.items—how many items to add to a
playerData[playeruuid].items
 * @param {number} data.monsters—how many slain monsters to
add to playerData[playeruuid].monsters
 */
CellarDweller.prototype.updatePlayerData = function(uuid, data) {
    // do the updating here
}
```

So far, so good! We're putting the data in an object because it makes it a little easier to scale if we want to start tracking more things besides itemCount and monsterCount. Now all we have to do is create a new property on our playerData object for each player, based on their uuid. The value of that property will be an object with items and monsters properties. Nice and simple! We just need to do a couple of checks to make sure that we're not trying to access properties that are undefined.

```javascript
CellarDweller.prototype.updatePlayerData = function(uuid, data) {
    if (this.playerData[uuid] !== undefined) {
        var currentData = this.playerData[uuid];
        // we can iterate over the properties in the data object
        for (var key in data) {
            if (data[key] !== undefined && typeof currentData[key]
            === number) {
                currentData[key] = currentData[key] + data[key];
            }
        }
    } else {
        // could put some checks hereto strictly enforce that data
        // can only contain monster and item properties
        this.playerData[uuid] = data;
    }
}
```

Another method crossed off the list! You've seen pretty much all of the code that's in there before. I tried to make it a little more generic, which has its pros and cons. We aren't enforcing that the data object only contains monsters and items. This is a little unsafe, but it'll let us scale to add other information.

The last thing we need to do is change our handleEntityDeath and handlePlayerPickup methods to get the necessary information and call our updatePlayerDataMethod. That'll look something like this:

```javascript
CellarDweller.prototype.handleEntityDeath = function(event) {
    // figure out if it's a monster
    var entity = event.entity;
    if (entity instanceof Java.type("org.bukkit.entity.Monster")) {
```

```
if (this.boxInfo.containsPoint(entity.location)) {
        this.totalMonsters -= 1;
        // start of updated code. Move player up here out of
the object scope because we use it in a couple places now
        var player = entity.getKiller();
         var info = {
        entity: entity,
        location: location,
        player: player,
         monster: entity.name,
         }
        EventDispatcher.dispatch(CellarDweller.
        MonsterSlayEvent, info);
        // update our playerData state
        this.updatePlayerData(player.getUniqueId(), {monsters:
        1});
    // end of updated code
        }
     }
     }
```

That's it! The only new method we're seeing here is player.
getUniqueId, which returns the player's UUID. No problem
at all! This stuff just keeps getting easier and easier, doesn't
it? Now it's time for you to go ahead and update your
handlePlayerPickupItem method in the same way and we're
home free. Now all we have to do is save our state when the
server shuts down.

# Being Persistent: Part 2— Saving State

 1   30–40 minutes

## Activity Overview

Lucky for us, ScriptCraft has another super useful module called persist, which automatically writes data to our computer's file system when the server shuts down, and loads it when the server starts back up. Rather than saving to a database, the module serializes our data structure to JSON—Javascript Object Notation, which is a very common format used for data transmission. Serialization is the process of converting a data structure or object to a format that can either be saved to a file or database, or transmitted—for instance, from a server to a client (the browser). Deserialization is the process of taking that serialized data and converting it back to the original data structure or object it derived from.

JSON is the format of choice for communication between back-end APIs and client apps. It's based on JavaScript, but it's actually not language dependent. All the major languages support JSON serialization and deserialization, either through standard libraries or modules.

It's worth noting that not everything is serializable (it looks like a made-up word, but it's not!) by the persist module. For instance, we can't serialize SpigotMC (Java) classes and methods. We're in pretty good shape, however, because all of our fields are just strings and numbers, which are easy to serialize.

We're going to write a static method that wraps the persist module in order to serialize all of our CellarDweller instances, including player data, so they can be saved when the server shuts down and loaded when the server starts back up.

# Instructions

To start, we have to require the persist module just like everything else:

```
// other requires are up here ^
var persist = require('persist');
```

We need to do one important thing to make this work. We need to provide each CellarDweller instance with a name and a UUID so we can load them from the file that gets saved. We should make the name a default parameter for in the constructor, so this requires a new argument (don't forget to update your JSDoc!):

```
// from this
var CellarDweller = function(location, w, h, options) { ...
// to this
var CellarDweller = function(name, location, w, h, options) { ...
// and then further down in the constructor
this.name = name;
```

Now we need to create a UUID. For that, we can use a Java static method to do that. Nashorn is great!

```
// somewhere in the constructor
var UUID = Java.type("java.util.uuid");
this.uuid = UUID.randomUUID().toString();
```

Excellent. Now all we have to do is save it! Let's write a method for that.

```
/**
 * A static method to persist all CellarDweller instances
 * @param {CellarDweller} cellarDweller—the CellarDweller instance
 * @static
```

```
*/
CellarDweller.save = function(cellarDweller) {
    var store = persist('cellar-dweller-data', {});
    store[cellarDweller.uuid] = cellarDweller;
}
```

Again this method isn't as bad as it looks. We call the persist function, which takes two arguments: the name of the file we want to save to, and the initial data structure that gets saved to the file when it's first written. If there's data in the file, it gets returned and stored in the store variable.

The persist function is using a static method called JSON. stringify under the hood, which will take all of our CellarDweller's properties (not methods, thankfully) and serialize them to a JSON string that can be written to a file. That should be enough information for us to be able to load everything in the next (and final!) activity.

# Being Persistent: Part 3: Loading State

 1  30–40 minutes

## Activity Overview

For the final activity, we're going to try loading a saved CellarDweller instance. Because we set its property name as a UUID, we're guaranteed not to overwrite any data. The only problem is that we really don't want to have to load a CellarDweller instance by its UUID, do we? It'd be nice if we could do it by name. What we can do is create a static load method that takes a name as its argument. Then, we can iterate over all of the saved CellarDweller instances and pull the one with the appropriate name!

# Instructions

Time to write our last method! Let's call it CellarDweller.load:

```
/**
* A static method to load all CellarDweller instances
* @param {string} name—the name of the CellarDweller instance
* @returns {(CellarDweller | null)}—returns the deserialized
CellarDweller instance if present in the store, otherwise returns null
* @static
*/
CellarDweller.load = function(name) {
    var store = persist('cellar-dweller-data', {});
    var result = null;
    for (var key in store) {
        var cellarDweller = store[key];
        if (cellarDweller.name === name) {
            result = cellarDweller;
            break;
        }
    }
    if (result === null) {
        return result;
    } else {
        // now what do we do with it?
    }
}
```

That's a pretty straightforward linear search. All we're doing is iterating over all of our store properties until we find a matching name. If it's null, we can return null. Otherwise, we can instantiate a new CellarDweller object with the properties from our loaded, deserialized instance.

```
// this is in our "else" scope
var cd = new CellarDweller(result.name, result.location,
result.w, result.h, result.options);
cd.uuid = result.uuid;
cd.floors = result.floors;
cd.boxInfo = new BoxInfo(result.location, result.w, result.h);
// now we have what we need
return cd;
```

We have to create a new BoxInfo instance because it has a bunch of useful methods that don't get serialized. Other than that, it's pretty straightforward. Now ops can resume their game(s) where they left off when the server shutdown. Awesome! FYI, here is the method in its entirety:

```
/**
 * A static method to load all CellarDweller instances
 * @param {string} name—the name of the CellarDweller instance
 * @returns {(CellarDweller | null)}—returns the deserialized
CellarDweller instance if present in the store, otherwise returns null
 * @static
 */
CellarDweller.load = function(name) {
        var store = persist('cellar-dweller-data', {});
        var result = null;
        for (var key in store) {
                var cellarDweller = store[key];
                if (cellarDweller.name === name) {
                        result = cellarDweller;
                        break;
                }
        }
        if (result === null) {
                return result;
        } else {
```

```javascript
        var cd = new CellarDweller(result.name, result.location,
        result.w, result.h, result.options);
        cd.uuid = result.uuid;
        cd.floors = result.floors;
        cd.boxInfo = new BoxInfo(result.location, result.w,
        result.h);
        // Now we have what we need
        return cd;
        }
    }
```

Well, that's all! You've successfully written a mod in just a few activities! Once you're done basking in the warm glow of that awesome accomplishment, you'll find out there's still plenty more to do. You'll likely notice some funny bugs (like monsters getting stuck in walls) and other little quirks in the code. This is all stuff that can be improved or built upon with a little bit of work. It may not be perfect, but you built it with your own two hands! Or at least your fingers. Now you have all of the tools you need to turn this into a major mod! You can deck out your dungeons with more stuff (cobwebs, bookshelves), add more interactivity via events, and save and load the state of the game. I really look forward to seeing a bunch of your mods popping up online!

# GLOSSARY

**abstracting** The concept of making code less complicated by hiding its inner workings in another function or class.

**accumulator** A programming pattern that updates a value with each iteration.

**anonymous functions** A function that has no name, which can be written inline; often used as callbacks.

**arguments** A comma-separated list of inputs provided to a function.

**arrays** Indexed collections of data composed of individual elements.

**assignment** Giving a value stored in memory a specific location in the memory register.

**asynchronous** Code that does not block the execution of a program until it is completed.

**callbacks** A function that is called after some code is executed; heavily used in event-driven programming.

**classes** A template for producing similar objects; defines the kinds of properties (i.e., values) and methods (i.e., functions) that its object instances may have.

**closure** A feature allowing programmers to keep a variable alive outside of its scope.

**compile time** The time period when a piece of software is compiled; syntax errors are caught during this stage.

**compilers** Computer programs that read all source code files and convert their instructions to a lower-level language such as assembly or native machine code.

**concatenation** The process of joining two objects together.

**constants** An immutable value that never changes (i.e. stays constant) throughout a program; typically named in all caps with words separated by underscores.

**declarative** A programming paradigm that is more concerned with what a block of code or function does, rather than how it is implemented.

**default** The value or behavior executed by a program when no other cases are satisfied.

**deserialization** The process of converting serialized data back into a programming language's native data structures.

**emitted** In event-driven programming, events are emitted, or dispatched usually based on some condition or user input;

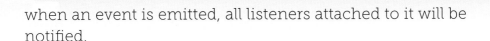

when an event is emitted, all listeners attached to it will be notified.

**encapsulation** A term used in object-oriented programing that refers to how a class can contain both properties (data, values) and methods (functions).

**entities** Refers to the base class of all living (or undead) things in the *Minecraft* world (SpigotMC/*Minecraft* specific).

**event handlers** A callback function supplied to an event listener to be called whenever the event occurs.

**event-driven** A programming paradigm where events are emitted or dispatched as a result of some type of input or user action; events are intercepted by listeners, which in turn execute a callback function.

**function** A reusable block of code that does something.

**functional programming** A programming paradigm based on the use of mathematical functions; characteristics include the use of immutable data structures, declarative semantics, and pure functions.

**higher-order functions** Functions that can be treated just like any other value in a program; key components of functional programming.

**IDE** Integrated development environment; a program that combines programming tools and a text editor.

**immutable** Unable to be changed once declared.

**imperative** A programming paradigm that uses statements to explicitly change a program's state.

**incrementation** The process of incrementing a number by one; denoted by the "++" operator.

**instance** A single occurrence of an object, which is an instance of a class.

**instantiate** To create an object by producing an instance of a class; instantiating an object is done by calling a class's constructor.

**interpreters** Computer programs that read source code line by line, converting the instructions to machine code and executing them immediately.

**iteration** The repetition of instructions while or until a condition is met; can also be called looping.

**JavaScript Object Notation** A text format that is often used to exchange data between systems; abbreviated JSON.

**key** A symbol (or label) mapped to a value in a dictionary; a label mapped to a property in an object data structure.

**lexical scope** Refers to a type of scoping that allows for variables to only be accessed within the function that they have been declared in.

**listeners** Functions that wait for an event to occur; functions attached, or subscribed, to a particular event.

**memory** The component of a computer that is responsible for storing information.

**modeling** The process of conceptually designing classes, often basing them off of real-world objects.

**mutability** A value's ability to be changed, or mutated.

**nested** Referring to blocks of code that are contained within another block of code.

**object literals** A syntactic feature of JavaScript that allows users to write objects literally; denoted by curly brackets.

**object-oriented** Describing a programming paradigm based on the use of objects and classes.

**objects** Single instances of classes; can have properties and methods and can contain state.

**object space** Refers to the coordinate space relative to an individual 3D object or model; all positions are in the local coordinate system.

**operands** The values that perform the computation symbolized by an operator.

**operators** Symbols that denote some type of computation in a programming language.

**persistence**  The act of saving state to be accessed beyond a program's execution life cycle.

**primitives**  The basic, fundamental types that a language provides.

**process**  The instance of a program that is currently running; a program can also create subprocesses.

**programming paradigm**  An organizational, structural, or philosophical principle governing how a program is written, based on a language's features; also considered a means of classifying a language.

**prototypes**  A set of methods and properties used to define objects and functions in JavaScript.

**prototypical inheritance**  The assignment of a set of methods and properties to an object based on a prototype.

**recursion**  When a function calls itself; used as an alternative to iteration.

**reflection**  The process of retrieving information about an object.

**return**  A value given by a function upon completion of its execution.

**runtime**  The time period when a piece of software is actually executed; semantic errors are caught during this stage.

**scoping** Refers to the visibility of variables within programs.

**semantics** The instructions that a compiler or interpreter translates to machine code; what a program actually means.

**serialization** Converting or translating data so it can be transmitted to another system.

**side effects** Changes to the state of a value outside the scope of a function.

**singleton** A programming pattern that allows for only a single instance of a class or object.

**spawn** Creating an instance of an entity and places it in the World (SigotMC/*Minecraft* specific).

**state** Refers to a program's variables and their values; also known as program state.

**static** A method that does not need access to the object instance.

**synchronous** Code that blocks the execution of a program until it is completed.

**syntax** The structure or grammar of a programming language.

**tags** A form of metadata that associates a term with a piece of data.

**tasks** Work (i.e., functions) that are scheduled in a task queue to be executed asynchronously in the background.

**ternary** An operator that allows programmers to write short-form conditional statements.

**transformation** Refers to the transformation of coordinates in one coordinate space to another.

**types** The different kinds of values a program can work with.

**universally unique identifier** A type of identifier that can be used as a unique key within a program.

**world space** Refers to the global coordinate space where several models and objects coexist.

# INDEX

## A

accumulator, 206, 207

anonymous functions, 116, 117, 119, 120, 122, 123, 183, 204

argument, 32, 39, 40, 41, 44, 90, 106, 108, 109, 113, 114, 120, 123, 127, 136, 179, 181, 202, 203, 204, 217, 222, 228, 229

arrays, 23–25, 26, 27–28, 35, 61, 76, 77, 78, 79, 80, 81, 85, 101, 102, 108, 109, 111, 113, 119, 121, 139, 140, 165, 166, 175, 176, 177, 187, 188, 190, 199, 202, 203, 204, 205, 206, 207, 208, 224

assignment, 16, 17, 22

asynchronous programming, 169, 180

## C

callback, 108–110, 115, 116, 119, 120, 121, 180, 206, 207, 208, 209, 210, 215, 221

classes, 7, 42, 43, 44, 45, 46, 69, 71, 73, 83, 109, 110, 111, 118, 124, 125–126, 127, 128, 130, 132, 134–136, 138, 143, 175, 211, 216, 227

closures, 125, 182, 183

compilers, 9, 13, 14, 15, 59

concatenation, 72, 73–74, 206

constants, 84, 100

## D

declarative programming, 92, 94, 160, 162, 163, 202, 203, 204, 228

default, 32, 33, 63, 83, 93, 99, 147, 155, 158, 198

deserialization, 227, 230, 231

doSpawn, 193, 194, 195, 196, 214, 215

## E

encapsulation, 125–126

# T

# U

# W

## About the Author

Joshua Romphf is the programmer for the River Campus Libraries' Digital Scholarship Lab at the University of Rochester, where he specializes in application development, video encoding, graphics programming, and physical computing. Romphf lends his expertise to several research projects on campus, spanning software development, fabrication, and electronics. He has taught video encoding and programming workshops to young adults at the L. Jeffrey Selznick School of Film Preservation, the University of Rochester, the University of Buffalo, the Digital Humanities Summer Institute, the University of Ottawa, and the RCADE Symposium at Rutgers, Camden.

## Photo Credits

Cover The Rosen Publishing Group/Wendy Dunning; cover, p. 1 (binary code) Valery Brozhinsky/Shuttertock.com; p. 54, 57, 67, 103, 109, 121, 140, 142, 156, 157, 169, 178, 201, 209, 210, 215, 218 by Joshua Romphf.

Design: Greg Tucker; Layout: Nicole Russo-Duca; Editor: Siyavush Saidian